THE GREAT AMERICAN
QUIZ BOOK

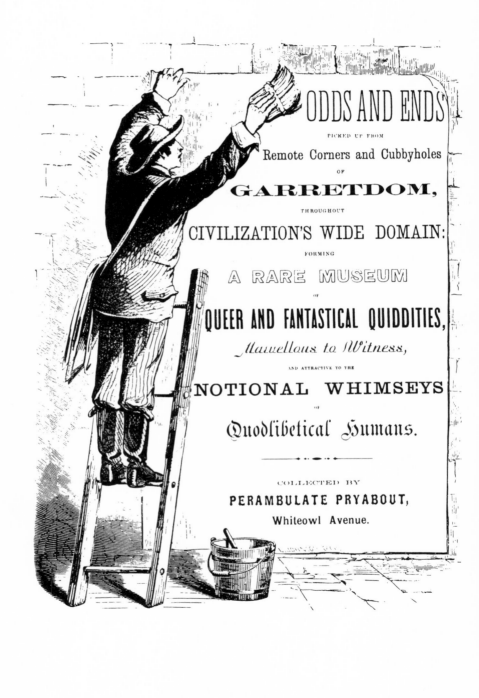

THE GREAT AMERICAN
QUIZ BOOK

BY
WILLIAM T. BULGER
FRANK O. RANGER

Pagurian Press Limited

NEW YORK   TORONTO

ISBN 0-88932-054-3 Cloth
0-88932-055-1 Paper
Printed and bound in the United States of America

to Kevin, Katherine, Mary, and Brian
and
to Marge and Ann

Contents

Preface

History, according to Arnold Toynbee, "is just one damned thing after another." Napoleon said that "History is a myth that men agree to believe." And then there was Henry Ford who said, "History is bunk!"

Whatever your definition, the questions and answers collected in this book represent insignificant and unimportant matters of history that are still fascinating in themselves. You will not find a discussion of the inevitability of the Civil War, the economic origins of the American Revolution, or the primary religious results of the Great Awakening. Instead, you will find the trifles of American history. You will learn some tidbits of information about famous Americans, infamous Americans, and about other people who are often ignored in the nation's history books.

The interest in trivia seems to go along with the cult of nostalgia that has grown in the past decade. Books on all sorts of trivia have poured from the presses. Although there are many trivia books on sports, movies, presidents, first facts, etc., there appears to be a need for a book dealing with the trivia of American history. So here it is. We hope that you will not think that it is bunk; instead, that as you read, you will discover "just one damned thing after another."

Introduction

The history of the European discovery of America begins with Christopher Columbus who didn't know just where he was going, didn't know where he was when he got there, and didn't know where he had been when he got back to Spain. Indeed, after four trips to the Americas, Columbus died without realizing that he had discovered a new world. If he was confused, things have become worse in the five hundred odd years since.

The history of the United States is the story of people — people who either came themselves or whose ancestors came here from Asia, Africa, and Europe. The ancestors of the American Indians began to arrive here 20,000 or 25,000 years ago. By the early 16th century, the Spaniards were exploring in what is now the United States. Black people arrived at Jamestown a year before the *Mayflower* docked at Plymouth.

In many cases, the facts about these people are more interesting than fiction. As we look at their accomplishments, failures, follies, and foibles, we learn about our past and we learn about ourselves.

Not all history is serious. George Washington, the Father of the Country, has been the butt of many jokes. Many people hear that term "Father of the Country" and believe that when Washington was sleeping in all those places up and down the east coast, he was never sleeping alone. Yet it seems likely that the General was sterile. His only children were Martha's grandchildren, whom he adopted. The insults hurled at him in his years as president, and the jokes told about him since then, have had little effect on his fame. Except for the fact that he wrote a love letter to the wife of his best friend, and the fact that in later life he disliked the actions of his mother, he remains a man of highest character.

If you would have a man of a more lusty character, look at Benjamin Franklin. It is easy to forget that he spent the first seventeen years of his life in Puritan Boston. He shed his Puritanism on his way to Philadelphia. And the religious teachings of the Quakers in the City of Brotherly Love did not affect him greatly. Franklin thought that religion was a fine thing — for other people. Like Washington, Jefferson, and Thomas Paine, Franklin remained a Deist.

Franklin was also a peculiar family man. He loved his wife but he spent years abroad away from her. He charmed the hearts of many ladies in London and Paris, as well as Philadelphia. John Adams was shocked to arrive in Paris and find· septuagenarian Franklin dallying with the aristocratic ladies.

The man who preached hard work and morality in the pages of *Poor Richard, An Almanack* set a different sort of example for his own family. He had an illegitimate son, William, whom he raised. When he married Deborah, the whereabouts of her first husband were unknown, so she and Franklin were married at common law, and not in the church. When William Franklin grew up, Benjamin eventually was able to have his boy appointed the Royal Governor of New Jersey. By this time, William had produced an illegitimate son of his own, whose upbringing was left largely to Grandpa.

During the Revolution, Franklin took his grandson, Temple, to Paris as his secretary. And what should Temple do but father a child by a Parisian girl, without benefit of clergy. This baby soon died and the illegitimate line of male Franklins ended (at least these were the only ones that Ben acknowledged). Imagine what the media would do with such a career today.

Thomas Jefferson is being charged with fathering five children by one of his slaves. The charges are still being debated, but Jefferson did free these five at his death. But our liberal third President did not free all his slaves in his will as many people believe. Jefferson was caught in the web of economic need, and slaves were money. Although Jefferson deplored slavery, he passed his slaves on down to his heirs. Indeed, only George Washington among the Founding Fathers provided in his will for the freedom of his slaves. And even in this instance, they were not to become free until after Martha's death.

As the United States entered the nineteenth century, people began to yearn for heroes. They couldn't very well use the old British heroes, so they had to invent their own. And what a job they did! Washington was transformed from a man of talent into a super-hero. Today it is difficult to think of him as a real man. Parson Weems was responsible for many of the myths about Washington, and many others helped the stories grow. Horatio Greenough carved a statue of the General as a Greek god in a toga. (Many people were shocked at this half-nude version and for years the statue was hidden in the back rooms of the Smithsonian.) Other artists portrayed the late President ascending bodily into heaven. And near his mother's home was placed a sign referring to "Mary, the mother of Washington" — an effort to make the old girl into a Protestant saint.

The nineteenth century also produced many other myths that are still with us. People were told that farmers were better than city people because the farmers worked with the soil and were somehow closer to their Creator. And the press informed the public that consolidation was perfectly all right for business but was absolutely wrong for labor. While the public was swallowing these stories, Horatio Alger came along and developed the rags to riches myth. People believed that if a boy came from a farm or emigrated from abroad, had little education, and started work at an early age, he would rise to the top in America. Lincoln, Garfield, Carnegie, and Henry Ford were used as examples, and Alger wrote over a hundred novels on the theme. Yet studies showed that the best way to attain a high position in American finance was to come from an urban, middle class family, one that had been in the country for several generations; get a good education, start work at an older age, and then work like hell. Most of the big business leaders at the turn of the century got ahead in this fashion.

As we look at our history, we find that even our presidents are human now and then. We have it on the authority of Harry Truman that President Chester Arthur kept a whore in the White House. Mr. Harding may not have kept one in the presidential mansion, but he had at least two mistresses. Franklin Roosevelt had an old girl friend with him at Warm Springs, Georgia, when he died. And recently the line of ladies claiming to have slept with John Kennedy is growing at an unbelievable rate.

14

President William McKinley had difficulties with another kind of Hoar — Senator George F. Hoar of Massachusetts. Mrs. McKinley was troubled by the Senator's surname and always tried to avoid using it. On one occasion Senator Hoar turned up at a White House reception without his wife. After greeting the President, he approached Mrs. McKinley. The First Lady saw him coming and said, "Good evening, Senator. Where is Mrs. 'W'?"

Calvin Coolidge slept a lot, but he caused no scandals. He also talked very little. Once before a White House dinner, the wife of a cabinet member bet her husband ten dollars that she could get the President to say at least three words. At the dinner, she happened to be seated next to Coolidge and she tried vainly to engage him in conversation. Finally as the dessert and coffee were being served, the lady decided on a new approach. Frankness seemed to be the only solution. She said, "Mr. President, I bet my husband ten dollars that I could get you to speak three words to me tonight." The President turned a bemused eye on her and replied, "You lose!"

Then there was William Howard Taft whose weight was a scandal. Taft hit the scales at between 330 to 350 pounds. Once at a press dinner where it was the custom to rib the President, Taft was introduced by Senator Chauncey Depew, a noted wit. Depew said, "It is my great honor and high privilege to introduce the President of the United States, the pregnant Mr. Taft." The President got up and responded. "Senator Depew has referred to me as the pregnant Mr. Taft. Well, if it is a girl I shall call her 'Clara' after that illustrious heroine of the Civil War, Clara Barton. And if it should be a boy, I shall call him 'Theodore' after my famous predecessor in the White House. But, if as I suspect, it is merely gas, I'll call it 'Chauncey Depew'."

Yet our history has a serious side. The Bicentennial made us aware of the great ability of our founding fathers and mothers. In 1776, with a population of three million, we were blessed with people like John and Abigail Adams, George Washington, Thomas Jefferson, Benjamin Franklin, Mercy Otis Warren, Benjamin Banneker, James Madison, Patrick Henry, and Alexander Hamilton, to name a few. Look what we have today with a population of over 210 million. The comparison is interesting!

So, we are dealing with people. The big things they did are in other books; the little things are here.

PRESIDENTIAL QUIZ

Q. Which president accepted the gift of the Statue of Liberty from France on October 28, 1886?

A. Grover Cleveland.

Q. Which president had a set of uncomfortable false teeth made from rhinoceros ivory?

A. George Washington.

Q. Which president often fell asleep after dinner and during conferences?

A. William Taft.

Q. Who did President Herbert Hoover order to drive the unemployed "Bances-Marchers" out of Washington in July, 1932?

A. General Douglas MacArthur, the Chief of Staff. MacArthur drove the marchers out and helped to reduce Hoover's slim chance for re-election.

Q. Was Lincoln a popular president when elected in 1860?

A. Not too popular. He received just under 40% of the popular vote. Although his three opponents together had nearly a million more popular votes than he had, Lincoln easily carried the Electoral College.

Q. Which president, facing court-martial, resigned from the army prior to the Civil War?

A. Ulysses S. Grant.

Q. What nineteenth-century president had a secret operation?

A. Grover Cleveland. In his second term, Cleveland developed a malignant growth in the top of his mouth. He pretended to go on vacation. To insure secrecy, the operation took place aboard a private yacht, the *Oneida*, in July, 1893. Although there were a few rumors about the operation, it was not publicly revealed until 1917 when one of the doctors talked.

Q. Which president traveled 50,000 miles and visited every state in the Union during his first term?

A. Theodore Roosevelt.

Q. What caused George Washington's death?

A. Washington caught a cold in December, 1799. At his request, the physicians bled him several times. The loss of blood was in large part the cause of his death.

Q. Which president, while working as an engineer, was trapped in China in the 1900 Boxer Rebellion?

A. Herbert Hoover.

Q. Which president carried off all the files of his administration when he left the White House?

A. Andrew Johnson.

Q. Who was the only president who was at one time a prisoner of war?

A. Andrew Jackson. During the Revolutionary War, Jackson and his brother, Robert, were captured by the British (April, 1781). The future President was only fourteen. Two weeks later both young men were released at the request of their mother.

Q. What was the great tragedy of President John Tyler's administration?

A. On February 28, 1844, the President took a number of guests for a gala cruise down the Potomac in a new steam frigate, the *Princeton*. Among the guests were cabinet members, congressmen, military officers, society people (including Dolley Madison). Also included were "Senator" David Gardiner and his daughters — one of whom, Julia, the President was hoping to marry. Just off Mount Vernon, a new gun, the Peacemaker, was fired. Although the gun had been fired several times earlier on the voyage, this time it exploded. Eight people were killed including Gardiner, the Secretary of State, and the Secretary of the Navy. Eleven people were wounded. The President and Julia were delayed below decks and their lives were spared.

Q. Which president called the official jet Columbine?

A. Dwight D. Eisenhower.

Q. Who called his jet The Spirit of 76?

A. Richard Nixon.

20

Q. What presidents received the Nobel Peace Prize?

A. Theodore Roosevelt and Woodrow Wilson. Although Roosevelt glorified war and despised pacifists, he reluctantly accepted the task of mediator in the Russo-Japanese War. He arranged a meeting between the warring sides at the naval yard near Portsmouth, New Hampshire. A peace treaty was signed. Roosevelt won the Nobel Prize in 1906. He was the first American to receive a Nobel Prize. Wilson received the Peace Prize in 1919 for his efforts in ending World War I and for promoting the League of Nations. The U. S. A., of course, never joined the League of Nations.

Q. What is the official name of the president's plane?

A. Air Force One.

Q. Princeton University has produced two American presidents. Who were they?

A. James Madison was a graduate of Princeton. So was Woodrow Wilson. John Kennedy attended Princeton for a short time but left due to illness. Kennedy, of course, later graduated from Harvard.

Q. Which president first received a salary of $50,000?
A. Ulysses S. Grant, beginning in his second term in 1873.

Q. Which president lost his Virginia estate to creditors and, after the death of his wife in 1830, moved to New York to live with his daughter?
A. James Monroe.

Q. What kind of voting experience did Ulysses S. Grant have before becoming president?
A. Grant had voted for president only once before he assumed the office himself. In his last message to Congress (December, 1876) he admitted this and apologized for his lack of political experience and for the errors made during his administration.

22

Q. Did George Washington really pray in the snow at Valley Forge?

A. Probably not. This story comes from Parson Weem's *Life of Washington*. At Valley Forge, Washington had a pleasant stone house as his headquarters. An Episcopalian, he did not take the sacrament because he did not believe in kneeling. It is highly unlikely that he knelt at Valley Forge.

Q. Which president first received a $75,000 salary?

A. William Taft in 1909.

Q. What president gave his name to tar-paper shacks and slums?

A. During the Depression of the 1930s, people living in shantytowns called their homes Hoovervilles. Newspapers used to cover people sleeping on park benches were referred to as Hoover's Blankets. It is ironic that Hoover's reputation was so bad. Earlier, he had been famous as the man who fed millions of Europeans during World War I.

Q. Who is Leslie Lynch King, Jr.?

A. This was President Gerald Ford's name at birth. He was later adopted by his stepfather and became Gerald Rudolph Ford.

Q. In three national elections, the presidential candidate with the largest popular vote lost the election. Who are the three men who lost these elections?

A. In 1824, Andrew Jackson won the popular vote but lost to John Quincy Adams in the House of Representatives; in 1876, Samuel Tilden was the choice of the people but lost to Rutherford B. Hayes; in 1888, Grover Cleveland took the popular vote but lost to Benjamin Harrison.

Q. One president studied medicine. Who was he?

A. William Henry Harrison, who studied medicine for a short time under the famous Philadelphia physician, Dr. Benjamin Rush.

Q. What was Daniel Webster's opinion of the vice-presidency?

A. When offered the nomination in 1848, Webster replied, "I do not propose to be buried until I am really dead." John Adams called the post "the most insignificant office that ever the inventions of man contrived."

Q. Who was the first president to make campaign speeches in a foreign language?

A. James Garfield, who made several speeches in German.

Q. Who was Edith B. Wilson?

A. Our only female president. Edith B. Wilson was Woodrow Wilson's second wife. She was a direct descendant of Pocahontas and John Rolfe. During her husband's illness from a stroke, she served, in effect, as the only woman president. She determined who was permitted to see Wilson and decided on what papers should be submitted to him.

Q. Who was the first First Lady to have graduated from college?

A. Lucy Hayes.

Q. One president had a vice-president who belonged to a different political party from that of the president. Who was he?

A. John Adams, a Federalist, had as his vice-president, Thomas Jefferson, a Republican.

Q. Where was the first presidential mansion?

A. No. 1 Cherry Street, New York City, occupied by President Washington from April 23, 1789 to February 23, 1790.

Q. Which president was such a fast reader that he often read several books a day?

A. Woodrow Wilson and John Kennedy were both rapid readers.

Q. Two future presidents signed the Constitution in 1787. Who were they?

A. George Washington, the President of the Convention, and James Madison, the Father of the Constitution.

Q. Which president's wife died between election day and his inauguration?

A. Andrew Jackson's.

Q. Which presidents tried to win re-election but failed?

A. John Adams, John Quincy Adams, Martin Van Buren, Grover Cleveland, Benjamin Harrison, William H. Taft, Herbert Hoover, and Gerald Ford. Cleveland eventually won a second term, but the terms were not consecutive. As a result he is counted twice when counting presidents.

Q. Two presidents were born in Vermont. Who were they?

A. Chester A. Arthur (near Fairfield) and Calvin Coolidge (Plymouth).

Q. Who was the first president to address Congress in over a hundred years?

A. Woodrow Wilson presented a message to Congress in person in 1913. This was the first address of a president to Congress since Jefferson ended the practice in 1801.

Q. Which president, on his first night in the White House, discovered that the trunk containing his personal belongings was still at the train depot?

A. Woodrow Wilson.

Q. Who was the youngest First Lady?

A. Frances Folsom Cleveland was twenty-one when she married President Grover Cleveland and became his First Lady in 1886.

Q. A number of U.S. presidents were descendants of kings. Who were they?

A. George Washington was descended from Henry III of England, Edward I, Edward II, and Edward III.

Thomas Jefferson was descended from David I, King of Scots.

James Monroe was descended from Edward III of England and Robert II, King of Scots.

John Quincy Adams was descended (through his mother) from Edward I, King of England.

William Henry Harrison and Benjamin Harrison were descended from Henry III of England.

Abraham Lincoln was descended from Edward I, King of England.

James Buchanan could trace his ancestry back to Robert II, King of Scots.

Ulysses Grant was descended from David I, King of Scots.

James Garfield was descended from Henry I, King of France, and Rhys Ap Tewdwr, King of Deheubarth.

Theodore Roosevelt was descended from Robert III, King of Scots.

William H. Taft was descended from David I, King of Scots.

Richard Nixon's ancestor was Edward III, King of England.

These relationships were worked out by Burke's, the famous English genealogists.

Q. How many presidents have testified before a Congressional Committee?

A. Three. Washington before the Senate seeking advice about a treaty; Lincoln twice — once to defend his wife against charges that she was a Confederate spy; and Ford, to defend his actions in pardoning Nixon.

Q. Which president vetoed the most bills?

A. Franklin Roosevelt, in the slightly more than twelve years he was in office, vetoed 631 bills; Grover Cleveland comes in second, vetoing 584 measures in eight years.

Q. How much formal education did Abraham Lincoln have?

A. In all, about one year. Lincoln developed his magnificent prose style through reading and through practice.

Q. Name the four presidents who were reared in parsonages.

A. Chester Arthur, Grover Cleveland, Woodrow Wilson, and Herbert Hoover.

Q. Which president's wife smoked a corncob pipe?

A. Rachel Jackson, Andrew Jackson's wife.

Q. What former president suffered a fatal stroke on the floor of the House of Representatives?

A. John Quincy Adams had an attack on February 21, 1848. He was carried to the Speaker's room where he went into a coma. He died two days later. His last words were: "This is the end of the earth, but I am composed." In some versions the word 'composed' is replaced with 'content'.

Q. What was Franklin Roosevelt's definition of a radical?

A. Roosevelt said: "A radical is a man with both feet firmly planted in the air."

Q. George Washington is related to a British sovereign and a famous Confederate general. Who are they?

A. Washington was a second cousin, seven times removed from Queen Elizabeth II, and a third cousin twice removed from General Robert E. Lee.

Q. Which president had to borrow money to attend his own inauguration?

A. George Washington.

Q. Whose books form the core of the Library of Congress?

A. Thomas Jefferson's. Congress bought 6700 volumes from Jefferson after the British burned the capital in 1814.

Q. Which two presidents and their wives celebrated their silver wedding anniversaries in the White House?

A. William Taft and Rutherford B. Hayes.

Q. Was there any relationship between George Washington and Sir Winston Churchill?

A. Yes, George Washington and Sir Winston were eighth cousins, six times removed.

Q. What has happened in the past century to presidents elected in a year ending in zero?

A. They have died in office. Harrison was elected in 1840 and he died in office. Lincoln was elected in 1860 and he died in office in his second term. Garfield, elected in 1880 died in office. McKinley, elected in 1900 for the second term died in office. Harding, elected in 1920 died in office. Franklin Roosevelt, elected in 1940 for the third time, died in office during his fourth term. Kennedy, elected in 1960, died in office. This gives the candidates of 1980 something to think about.

Q. Which president's wife was not born in the U.S.A.?

A. John Quincy Adams's. His wife, Louisa, was born in London.

Q. Who was the most famous dog ever to live in the White House?

A. Fala, Franklin Roosevelt's black Scottie.

Q. What president, on his way to Washington for his inauguration, saw his son (and only surviving child) killed by a train right before his eyes?

A. Franklin Pierce. Mrs. Pierce was also present.

Q. Which president's mother lived in the White House with him?

A. James Garfield's.

Q. What was the outcome of Thomas Hart Benton's duel with Andrew Jackson?

A. In September, 1813, Benton and Jackson engaged in a shooting brawl in downtown Nashville. Jackson fell with a shattered shoulder and a bullet in his arm. Jackson's friends then wounded Benton five times with daggers. This incident convinced Benton that he had better leave Tennessee. He moved to Missouri where in 1820 he was elected one of the state's first senators. In December, 1821, Benton and Jackson were both U.S. senators and had adjacent seats. They soon made up their quarrel and became lifelong friends.

Q. Who was the first president to lie in state in the Capitol Rotunda?

A. Abraham Lincoln.

Q. Did George Washington really cut down a cherry tree?

A. In his long life, Washington may very well have cut down a cherry tree, but the traditional account is fictional. It appears in the fifth edition of Parson Mason L. Weem's *Life of Washington*. Even here, Washington did not cut down the tree — he barked it severely.

32

Q. Which president's daughter eloped with Jefferson Davis?

A. Zachary Taylor's. Davis married Taylor's daughter in 1835, before Taylor was president. Mrs. Davis died within a few months of the marriage.

Q. What president is credited with introducing the spoils system?

A. Andrew Jackson — but Thomas Jefferson earlier practiced a similar system but not on so grand a scale.

Q. How did Alice Roosevelt Longworth describe President Calvin Coolidge?

A. She said that Coolidge "looked like he had been weaned on a pickle." Mrs. Longworth denied making up this *bon mot* but she circulated it.

Q. Who was the youngest president of the United States and who was the oldest?

A. The youngest was Theodore Roosevelt, who was 42 when he was inaugurated. The oldest was William Henry Harrison, who took the oath when he was 68 — and died a month later.

Q. Some Cabinets have been given special names. What are these?

A. Andrew Jackson had a Kitchen Cabinet, made up of friends who supposedly met in the kitchen of the White House. President Theodore Roosevelt had a Tennis Cabinet. Under President Harding, there was a Poker Cabinet. Herbert Hoover had a Medicine Ball Cabinet. Franklin Roosevelt had The Brain Trust, made up mostly of people outside the official Cabinet.

Q. Who issued the first presidential amnesty?

A. Abraham Lincoln on December 8, 1863.

Q. Who said "the world must be made safe for democracy"?

A. Woodrow Wilson in his speech to Congress, April 2, 1917, when he asked for a declaration of war against Germany.

Q. Which presidents were elected by the House of Representatives?

A. The House of Representatives has twice elected a president of the United States. This first occurred with Thomas Jefferson in 1801, and the second incident concerned the election of John Quincy Adams in 1825. The House *and* the Senate elected Gerald Ford as vice-president as provided by the Twenty-fifth Amendment.

Q. At what time have the most presidents been alive?

A. In March, 1861, when Abraham Lincoln was inaugurated, there were five ex-presidents alive — Van Buren, Tyler, Pierce, Fillmore, and Buchanan.

Q. Who was the first president to live in the White House?

A. John Adams, who moved into the unfinished building in 1800.

Q. One vice-president of the United States was elected by the Senate. Who was he?

A. Richard Johnson. In 1836, Johnson received only a plurality of the votes for vice-president. The Senate had to decide the election. Gerald Ford and Nelson Rockefeller were elected to the vice-presidency by *both* houses of Congress.

Q. Two presidents are buried in Arlington National Cemetery. Who are they?

A. William H. Taft and John F. Kennedy.

Q. Since 1937, when does the inauguration of a president take place?

A. The Twentieth Amendment to the Constitution, adopted in 1933, provides that the president elect shall begin his term on January 20. Prior to 1937, the president was inaugurated on March 4 unless the 4th fell on a Sunday, in which case he was sworn in on the following day.

Q. Who was the youngest president ever elected to that office?

A. John F. Kennedy was 43 when he became president. Theodore Roosevelt was only 42 when he took office but he had been elected to the vice-presidency, not the presidency.

Q. Which president was impeached by the House of Representatives but found not guilty by the Senate?

A. Andrew Johnson in 1868.

Q. Who was the first veteran of the Navy to become president?

A. John F. Kennedy.

Q. What ex-president was shot by an assassin but survived because the bullet passed through his glasses case and a speech manuscript?

A. Theodore Roosevelt was shot in the chest while campaigning on the Bull Moose ticket in Milwaukee in 1912. Upon finding that his lung was not punctured, Roosevelt went on with his speech. He referred to the man who tried to kill him as "You poor creature." He spoke for an hour to the amazement of his listeners. When he finally went to the doctors, they found the bullet four inches inside his chest — and left it there.

Q. We once had three presidents within a month. When did this occur?

A. In 1841. Martin Van Buren left office on March 4, the day that William H. Harrison was inaugurated. Harrison died on April 4 and was succeeded by John Tyler.

Q. Which president set the record for staying away from his job in the nation's capital?

A. John Adams, who was away for better than a year (385 days) of the four years that he was president. Adams spent most of his time at his home in Quincy, Massachusetts.

Q. In the past century, only five presidents have failed to win re-election. Who were they?

A. Cleveland, Benjamin Harrison, Taft, Hoover, and Ford.

Q. In the first fifty years of our history no president died in office. Who was the first to do so?

A. William Henry Harrison in 1841.

Q. What nineteenth century president wrote a best-selling book that brought in royalties of $450,000?

A. Ulysses S. Grant finished his two volumes of memoirs just a week before he died. He was deeply in debt but his writings saved his family.

Q. Meriwether Lewis, of the famous Lewis and Clark expedition to the Pacific coast, once served as the private secretary to what president?

A. From 1801 to 1803, Lewis was Thomas Jefferson's private secretary.

Q. Which president saw his wife accused of treason during wartime?

A. Mary Todd Lincoln was from Kentucky and she had relatives in both the Union and Confederate armies. People in and out of government accused her of favoring the Confederate cause and even of being a spy. When a congressional committee was investigating some of these charges against Mrs. Lincoln, the President made a surprise appearance to denounce the accusations.

Q. A president was once attacked by a would-be assassin who fired two guns at point-blank range. Who was he?

A. Andrew Jackson was attacked in 1835. His life was spared because both pistols misfired.

Q. In the 1950s, a movie, *The President's Lady,* **dealt with the life of what president and his wife?**

A. The film depicted the life of Andrew and Rachel Jackson.

Q. What president lingered seventy-nine days before dying of an assassin's bullet?

A. James Garfield was hit by one of the two bullets fired at him by Charles J. Guiteau. Doctors were unable to locate the bullet. They kept him in bed and continually probed with their germ-infected instruments, spreading disease through the President's body. The bullet was actually lodged in his back and the body created a protective cyst about it. The doctors, not the bullet, killed Garfield.

Q. In 1950, an assassination attempt was made on the president by Puerto Rican nationalists. Who was the president?

A. The attack was made against Harry Truman who was living in Blair House while the White House was being reconstructed. President Truman was not injured but a secret service man and one would-be assassin were killed.

Q. Which president won a Pulitzer Prize for literature?

A. John Kennedy received the award for his book, *Profiles in Courage*.

Q. What president was the first to visit the People's Republic in China?

A. Richard Nixon.

Q. The faces of four presidents are carved into the stone of Mount Rushmore, South Dakota. Who are they?

A. Presidents Washington, Jefferson, Lincoln, and Theodore Roosevelt.

Q. The twelfth president was a second cousin of the fourth president. Who were these two presidents?

A. Zachary Taylor and James Madison.

Q. Which president was sworn into office by his father?

A. Calvin Coolidge.

Q. A motion picture, *PT 109,* **depicted the naval career of what president?**

A. The film dealt with the early life of John F. Kennedy during his exploits in the Pacific in World War II.

Q. Robert Todd Lincoln, the eldest son of Abraham Lincoln, served as Secretary of War under what president?

A. He was Secretary of War from 1881 to 1885. Robert T. Lincoln was appointed to this office by President Garfield and continued to serve under President Arthur. Benjamin Harrison appointed Lincoln Minister to Great Britain.

Q. Who served as President Jefferson's hostess at all official functions?

A. Dolley Madison, the wife of the Secretary of State, served as Mr. Jefferson's hostess, since he was a widower. Mrs. Madison continued to be a pillar of Washington society, not only during her husband's two terms as president, but until her death in 1849.

Q. Which president lived the longest?

A. John Adams, who died at 90.

Q. Who was the first president to broadcast by radio?

A. Warren Harding. His speech at the dedication of the Francis Scott Key Memorial, Fort McHenry, Baltimore, Maryland, on June 14, 1922, was broadcast by WEAR of Baltimore.

Q. Which president's wife acted as his private secretary?

A. James Polk's.

Q. **Which two signers of the Declaration of Independence later became president?**

A. John Adams and Thomas Jefferson.

Q. **Which president died the youngest?**

A. John Kennedy, who was assassinated at the age of 46.

Q. **Who was the first president to pitch a baseball to open the baseball season?**

A. William Howard Taft, April 14, 1910. He threw the ball which opened the American League Washington-Philadelphia game.

Q. **Who was shot at the Baltimore and Potomac railroad station in Washington?**

A. James Garfield.

Q. **Which presidents won seats in Congress after they left the White House?**

A. John Quincy Adams was elected to the House of Representatives and served there for seventeen years. Andrew Johnson was elected to the Senate. John Tyler served in the Confederate House of Representatives. (Tyler was in the provisional House, but died before he could take his seat in the regular House.)

Q. **Which future president once resigned from the Senate because his wife hated living in Washington?**

A. Franklin Pierce.

42

Q. Who was the first president to broadcast from a foreign country?

A. Franklin Delano Roosevelt made a speech at Cartagena, Colombia, on July 10, 1934, which was relayed to New York and then rebroadcasted.

Q. Which president gave the bride away at the wedding of a future president?

A. Theodore Roosevelt, at the wedding of Franklin Roosevelt and Eleanor.

Q. Which president once had his clothes stolen while he was swimming in the Potomac River?

A. John Quincy Adams.

Q. Which president's wife was both the wife and mother of an American president?

A. Abigail Adams, wife of John.

Q. Which president apparently needed a great deal of rest, sleeping an average of eleven hours a day?
A. Calvin Coolidge.

Q. Who was the first president married in the White House?
A. Grover Cleveland was married to his ward, Frances Folsom, June 2, 1886.

Q. Who was the first mother of a president to see her son's inauguration?
A. Mr. James Garfield.

Q. Who was the first president to become a senator?
A. Andrew Johnson, the seventeenth president.

Q. Which president admitted to fathering an illegitimate child?
A. Grover Cleveland.

Q. Who was the first president married while in office?
A. John Tyler, the tenth president, 1841-1845. He married Julia Gardiner, daughter of a New York State senator on June 25, 1844.

Q. Who was the first president to broadcast in a foreign language?

A. Franklin Delano Roosevelt, who addressed the French people on November 2, 1942, from Washington, D.C.

Q. Who killed Charles Dickinson in a duel on June 5, 1806?

A. Andrew Jackson.

Q. Which president took the oath of office on an airplane?

A. Lyndon Johnson on *Air Force One*, shortly after the assassination of John F. Kennedy.

Q. Which president had the most children?

A. John Tyler had fifteen children by two wives; William Henry Harrison had ten.

Q. Who was often called the First Lady of the World?

A. Eleanor Roosevelt, wife of Franklin Roosevelt.

Q. Who was president when the "Star Spangled Banner" officially became our national anthem?

A. Herbert Hoover. It was adopted by an Act of Congress in 1931.

Q. Which two signers of the Constitution later became president?

A. George Washington and James Madison.

Q. Which former president swore two of his successors into office?

A. William Howard Taft, who became Chief Justice of the Supreme Court in 1921, swore in Calvin Coolidge in 1925 and Herbert Hoover in 1929.

Q. While the White House was being remodeled, which president and his wife lived at Blair House for three and a half years?

A. Harry and Bess Truman.

Q. Who were the last two presidents to go directly from the Senate to the White House?

A. Warren Harding and John Kennedy.

Q. Which president went directly from the House of Representatives to the White House?

A. James Garfield.

Q. Which First Lady planned the planting of the magnificent cherry trees around the Tidal Basin?

A. Helen Taft, wife of William.

Q. Who was the first president born on Independence Day?

A. Calvin Coolidge, the thirtieth president, was born on July 4, 1872, in Plymouth, Vermont.

Q. Who was the first president born beyond the boundaries of the original thirteen states?

A. Abraham Lincoln, the sixteenth president, was born in Hodgenville, Kentucky, on February 12, 1809.

Q. Who was the first president born a citizen of the United States?

A. Martin Van Buren, the eighth president (1837-41), was born on December 5, 1782, in Kinderhook, New York. Earlier presidents were born while the country was part of the British Empire.

Q. Who was the first president elected under the Constitution?

A. George Washington.

Q. Who was the first president buried in Washington, D.C.?

A. Woodrow Wilson, the twenty-eighth president, was buried on February 5, 1924, in the National Cathedral of the Protestant Episcopal Cathedral of Saints Peter and Paul.

Q. Which former president (1841-45) was a member of the Confederate Congress between 1861 and 1862?

A. John Tyler.

Q. Mamie Geneva Doud married which future president in 1916?

A. Dwight D. Eisenhower.

Q. What Union general opposed President Lincoln in 1864?

A. George McClellan.

Q. Which president is reputed to have been Aaron Burr's illegitimate son?

A. Martin Van Buren, according to John Quincy Adams's diary. The novelist, Gore Vidal, has used this tidbit in two novels, *Burr* and *1876*.

Q. How did Grover Cleveland avoid the draft?

A. Cleveland was a young lawyer when the Civil War began. Although two of his brothers entered the service, he hired a substitute so that he could work and support his widowed mother. This was a perfectly legal action at the time. When he ran for president in 1884, Cleveland was denounced as a draft dodger. His backers had a quick reply — his opponent, James G. Blaine, had hired a substitute too. John D. Rockefeller, who had just begun his successful business career when the war started, also hired a substitute.

Q. What president appointed his brother Attorney General?

A. John F. Kennedy.

Q. Who was the first president inaugurated on January 20th, in accordance with the Twentieth Amendment to the Constitution?

A. Franklin Delano Roosevelt was inaugurated for his second term on January 20, 1937, in Washington, D.C.

Q. This First Lady was once president of the American Girl Scouts. Who was she?

A. Lou Hoover, wife of Herbert.

Q. Who was the only president to be elected for a fourth term?

A. Franklin Delano Roosevelt, the thirty-second president, 1933-45. He was also the first president in the United States to be elected to a third term.

Q. Who lost the disputed 1876 election to Rutherford B. Hayes?

A. Samuel Tilden.

Q. Why was Mrs. Rutherford B. Hayes known as Lemonade Lucy?

A. Mrs. Rutherford B. Hayes, from 1877 to 1881, refused to permit wine or spirits to be served at White House dinners or receptions, substituting lemonade.

Q. What former vice-president ran for president on a minor party ticket in 1948?

A. Henry Wallace, as the candidate of the Progressive Party.

Q. Who was the first president to receive fewer popular and electoral votes than an opponent?

A. John Quincy Adams, the sixth president, 1825-29. In the November, 1824 elections, Andrew Jackson received more popular and electoral votes than did Adams. Because none of the four candidates had a majority of electoral votes, the House of Representatives decided the election among the top three candidates — Adams, Jackson, and William Crawford.

Q. Who lost to Franklin D. Roosevelt in 1944?

A. Thomas E. Dewey.

Q. Did General Grant demand the surrender of General Lee's sword?

A. Contrary to popular belief, this incident did not occur. In his *Memoirs*, Grant described the occasion. He wrote: "The much talked of surrendering of Lee's sword and my handing it back, this and much more that has been said about it is the purest romance."

Q. Who was the first president to visit a foreign country in wartime?

A. Franklin Delano Roosevelt flew from Miami to Trinidad, January 10, 1943.

Q. Who was the only president whose grandson became president also?

A. William Henry Harrison, the ninth president, 1841. His grandson, Benjamin Harrison was the twenty-third president, 1888-1893.

Q. Whose Cabinet was sarcastically called "nine millionaires and a plumber"?

A. Eisenhower's first Cabinet. Martin Durkin, the plumber, resigned less than a year after his appointment.

Q. Who was the first Catholic president in the United States?

A. John F. Kennedy, inaugurated January 20, 1961, thirty-fifth president.

Q. Which president once hanged a man?
A. Grover Cleveland, while Sheriff of Erie County, New York.

Q. Who was the first bachelor president?
A. James Buchanan, the fifteenth president, 1857-61.

Q. What were the Fireside Chats?
A. Franklin D. Roosevelt was the first president to appreciate the political potential of the radio. In his addresses from the fireside of the White House, he seemed to be talking directly to each family in their own living room. These radio addresses were obviously helpful to him politically — he was elected to the presidency four times.

Q. Which president was so fussy about details that he often insisted on answering the White House phone himself?

A. Grover Cleveland.

Q. Who was the first president to visit Europe while president?

A. Woodrow Wilson in 1918.

Q. Who won the Lincoln-Douglas debates in 1858?

A. Steven A. Douglas narrowly won re-election to the Senate, but he was no longer the unquestioned leader of his party, or the idol of the North. Abraham Lincoln, a new and towering figure, had been projected into the political scene. Senators were then elected by state legislatures. More people voted for Lincoln's supporters than for supporters of Douglas, but the legislature chose Douglas.

Q. Which fascinating First Lady saved many important state papers from destruction when the British burned the White House in 1814?

A. Dolley Madison.

Q. Who was the only president whose son became president also?

A. John Adams, the second president, 1797-1801, father of John Quincy Adams, the sixth president, 1825-1829.

Q. Which president was so rotund that he reportedly got stuck in the White House tub?

A. William H. Taft. An extra large tub was installed.

Q. Many of our presidents appear on the face of United States coins and savings bonds. Do you know which presidents appear on these coins — penny, nickel, dime, quarter, half-dollar, silver dollar?

A. Lincoln, Jefferson, F. Roosevelt, Washington, Kennedy, Eisenhower.

Q. Who was the first president to visit a foreign country while president?

A. Theodore Roosevelt sailed on the U.S.S. *Louisiana* from Panama, where he remained from November 14 to 17, 1906. From there he went to Puerto Rico.

Q. Which president was swindled by a business partner and was forced to pawn his private possessions for a loan?

A. Ulysses S. Grant.

Q. Which president never drew his salary until he retired from office?

A. Martin Van Buren.

Q. Who was the first child born in the White House as the offspring of a president?

A. The first child was Esther Cleveland, born September 9, 1893. She was the second child of Grover Cleveland and Frances, who were married June 26, 1886 in the Blue Room of the White House.

Q. Which president received the entire electoral vote?

A. George Washington — twice.

Q. When is Election Day?

A. The first Tuesday after the first Monday in November.

Q. When an attempt was made on Franklin D. Roosevelt's life on February 15, 1933, in Miami, Florida, who died instead?

A. Anton Cermak, Mayor of Chicago.

Q. Which presidents' faces appear on these U.S. Savings bonds: $25, $50, $75, $100, $200, $500, $1,000, $10,000?

A. The faces of Washington, Jefferson, Kennedy, Cleveland, F. Roosevelt, Wilson, Lincoln, T. Roosevelt.

Q. Which president had no children of his own, but adopted a nephew and an Indian boy?

A. Andrew Jackson.

Q. How many war presidents has the United States had? Who were they, and during which wars?

A. Lincoln—U.S. Civil War   Wilson—World War I
Madison—War of 1812   F. Roosevelt—World War II
Polk—Mexican War   Truman—Korean War
McKinley—Spanish   Johnson and Nixon —
American War   Vietnam War

Q. The oldest vice-president was a Kentuckian who served under Truman. Who was he?

A. Alben Barkley.

Q. How many presidents has the United States had? Can you name them?

A. Thirty-nine. They are:

George Washington	James A. Garfield
John Adams	Chester A. Arthur
Thomas Jefferson	Grover Cleveland
James Madison	Benjamin Harrison
James Monroe	William McKinley
John Quincy Adams	Theodore Roosevelt
Andrew Jackson	William Howard Taft
Martin Van Buren	Woodrow Wilson
William Henry Harrison	Warren G. Harding
John Tyler	Calvin Coolidge
James Knox Polk	Herbert Hoover
Zachary Taylor	Franklin D. Roosevelt
Millard Fillmore	Harry Truman
Franklin Pierce	Dwight D. Eisenhower
James Buchanan	John F. Kennedy
Abraham Lincoln	Lyndon B. Johnson
Andrew Johnson	Richard M. Nixon
Ulysses S. Grant	Gerald Ford
Rutherford B. Hayes	Jimmy Carter

Q. Which president did not change his Cabinet at all during his four years in the White House?

A. Franklin Pierce.

Let her bang, ye Heroes! Victory is Ours!

Q. What state has furnished the most presidents? What state is second?

A. *Virginia — eight*

George Washington	William H. Harrison
Thomas Jefferson	John Tyler
James Madison	Zachary Taylor
James Monroe	Woodrow Wilson

Ohio — seven

Ulysses S. Grant	William McKinley
Rutherford B. Hayes	William H. Taft
James A. Garfield	Warren G. Harding
Benjamin Harrison	

Q. What president was almost illiterate until his wife helped him to learn to read and write?

A. Andrew Johnson married Eliza McCardle when he was eighteen. He had begun to learn to read while a tailor's apprentice at fourteen. His wife encouraged him with his self-education. He improved his reading and learned to write. She also encouraged him to become a public speaker and a politician.

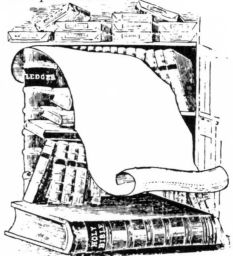

Q. Two presidents died on July 4, 1826. Who were they?

A. John Adams and Thomas Jefferson, both of whom had helped draft and had signed the Declaration of Independence, died exactly fifty years after the signing of that famous document.

Q. Where was the first presidential inauguration held?

A. In Federal Hall in New York City on April 30, 1789. Washington's second administration began in Congress Hall in Philadelphia on March 4, 1793. Thomas Jefferson, in 1801, was the first president to be inaugurated in Washington, D.C.

Q. **What does the "S" stand for in Harry S. Truman?**

A. For nothing. Truman simply added the initial.

Q. **On February 15, 1933, an assassination attempt was made on the life of president-elect Franklin D. Roosevelt. What happened?**

A. An unemployed bricklayer, Guiseppe Zangara, who hated public officials and the rich, sprayed bullets at Roosevelt and his entourage at a park in Miami, Florida. Roosevelt was unhurt but five of his party were wounded, Mayor Anton Cermak of Chicago fatally.

Q. **The capital city of Liberia is named for which American president?**

A. Monrovia is named for James Monroe.

Q. **What president sent troops to Little Rock, Arkansas, to uphold a court order to integrate the public schools?**

A. In September, 1957, Dwight Eisenhower ordered in 1,000 paratroopers and federalized over 10,000 National Guards to carry out the orders of the court.

Q. **How many states are named for a president?**

A. Only one, the state of Washington. Washington's name has also been given to seven mountains, eight streams, nine colleges, ten lakes, thirty-three counties, and 121 towns and villages.

Q. **How many guns are required for a presidential salute?**

A. The president rates a twenty-one gun salute. So does an ex-president and a president-elect.

Q. Whom did Thomas Jefferson marry?

A. Mr. Jefferson married a wealthy widow, Martha Wayles Skelton, on January 1, 1772. He was twenty-eight; she was twenty-three. A year after the marriage, her father died, leaving her forty-thousand acres of land and 135 slaves. But she also inherited some of her father's large debts, which caused Jefferson great financial difficulties later on. Mrs. Jefferson died in 1782, after having six children, three of whom died in infancy. Indeed, of the three surviving children, only one, Martha, outlived her father.

Q. Which president made the shortest inaugural address?

A. George Washington's second inaugural address on March 4, 1793, holds the record for brevity. It contained a total of 134 words.

Q. Who was the first president to speak on television?

A. On April 30, 1939, Franklin Roosevelt spoke over WNBT at the opening ceremony of the New York World's Fair.

Q. What president held a private pilot's license?

A. Dwight Eisenhower.

Q. Who said, "A House divided against itself cannot stand"?

A. Abraham Lincoln said this during his campaign for the Senate in Illinois in 1858.

Q. Who began the custom of observing Thanksgiving on the last Thursday in November?

A. Thanksgiving had been held earlier to commemorate various special occasions. In October, 1863, President Abraham Lincoln issued a proclamation calling on the people to set aside the last Thursday in November as a day of Thanksgiving.

Q. One president used to write out his speeches in short-hand and then type them himself. Who was he?

A. Woodrow Wilson.

Q. Which president declined a salary?

A. George Washington. The Congress paid it to him anyway. He had suggested in his first inaugural address that he merely be paid for his expenses.

Q. Who was the first president to ride in an automobile or an airplane?

A. Theodore Roosevelt. In 1902 he was a passenger in an electric automobile in Hartford, Connecticut. On October 11, 1910, he took an airplane ride in St. Louis, Missouri. At the time of the plane ride, Roosevelt was an ex-president.

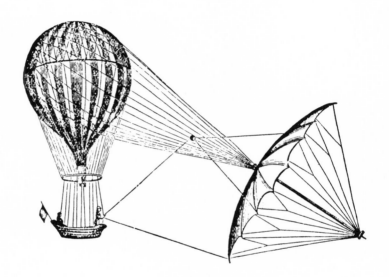

Q. What president was accused of having a daughter by his mistress, Nan Britton?

A. Warren Harding.

Q. What president suggested that our money system be based on the decimal system and the dollar?

A. Thomas Jefferson wrote a paper in April, 1784, suggesting such a system.

Q. Who is the only president to serve as Chief Justice of the United States after his term was ended?

A. William Howard Taft served as Chief Justice from 1921 to 1930.

Q. What president once helped to dissemble a core of a damaged nuclear reactor?

A. Jimmy Carter, while in the U.S. Navy helping to develop the first atomic powered submarine, was sent to Chalk River, Canada, to assist in removing the core of a nuclear reactor that had gone out of control and melted. The radiation level was so intense that Carter and his colleagues could work on the core for only 90 seconds at a time.

Q. What president used his nickname instead of his real name for all official business?

A. Although Grant, Cleveland, Wilson, Coolidge, Eisenhower, and Ford changed their names from the ones given at birth, Jimmy Carter (James Earl Carter, Junior), is the first president to use his nickname on official documents.

Q. The following quotations were made by U.S. presidents. Who is the president connected with each quotation?

"Ask not what your country can do for you — ask what you can do for your country."
A. John F. Kennedy.

"In this job, I'm not worried about my enemies. I can take care of them. It is my friends who are giving me trouble."
A. Warren G. Harding.

"He serves his party best who serves his country best."
A. Rutherford B. Hayes.

"The law is the only sure protection of the weak and the only efficient restraint upon the strong."
A. Millard Fillmore.

"We have the opportunity to move, not only toward the rich society and the powerful society, but upward to the great society."
A. Lyndon Johnson.

"I'm fit as a bull moose."
A. Theodore Roosevelt.

"We cannot escape history."
A. Abraham Lincoln.

"A little rebellion now and then is a good thing; the tree of liberty must be refreshed from time to time with the blood of patriots and tyrants."
A. Thomas Jefferson.

"Mankind must put an end to war or war will put an end to mankind."
A. John F. Kennedy.

"I shall go to Korea."
A. Dwight Eisenhower.

"We must be the great arsenal of democracy."
A. Franklin D. Roosevelt.

"There is no right to strike against the public safety by anybody, anywhere, anytime."
A. Calvin Coolidge.

"The basis of our political system is the right of the people to make and to alter their constitutions of government."
A. George Washington.

"With malice toward none, with charity for all."
A. Abraham Lincoln.

"While I can make no claim to having introduced the term 'rugged individualism,' I should be proud to have invented it."
A. Herbert Hoover.

"If you can't stand the heat, get out of the kitchen."
A. Harry Truman.

"The only thing we have to fear is fear itself."
A. Franklin Roosevelt.

"A public office is a public trust."
A. Grover Cleveland.

Q. Can you match the following presidents with their earlier occupations?

1. Dwight Eisenhower   A. President of Princeton University
2. Herbert Hoover   B. U.S. Minister to Holland, Prussia, Russia, and Great Britain
3. Harry Truman   C. Mayor of Buffalo, N.Y.
4. Grover Cleveland   D. President of Columbia University
5. Woodrow Wilson   E. President of Hiram College
6. Theodore Roosevelt and Franklin Roosevelt   F. Secretary of State under Madison
7. William H. Taft   G. Editor of a newspaper
8. John Q. Adams   H. Engineer
9. James Polk and Andrew Jackson   I. Surveyor
10. George Washington   J. Tailor
11. Calvin Coolidge   K. Professional soldier
12. Warren G. Harding   L. Governor of Massachusetts
13. Zachary Taylor, Ulysses S. Grant, and Dwight Eisenhower   M. Governor of Tennessee
14. Andrew Johnson   N. Governor-General of the Philippines
15. James Monroe   O. Proprietor of a clothing store
16. James Garfield   P. Victor of the Battle of New Orleans
17. Andrew Jackson   Q. Assistant Secretary of the Navy

A. 1. D   6. Q   10. I   14. J
    2. H   7. N   11. L   15. F
    3. O   8. B   12. G   16. E
    4. C   9. M   13. K   17. P
    5. A

Q. Below are listed the homes or vacation spots of a number of presidents. Which president do you associate with each place?
  1. The Hermitage
  2. Mount Vernon
  3. Montpelier
  4. Sherwood Forest, Charles City County, Virginia
  5. Spiegel Grove, Fremont, Ohio
  6. Monticello
  7. A ranch on the Pedernales River, Texas
  8. Wheatland, Lancaster, Pennsylvania
  9. The Summer White House, Key West, Florida
  10. San Clemente, California
  11. Hyde Park
  12. Gettysburg, Pennsylvania
  13. Sagamore Hill, Oyster Bay, Long Island
  14. Lindenwald, Kinderhook, N.Y.
  15. Hyannisport, Massachusetts
  16. Ash Lawn
  17. The Beeches, Northampton, Massachusetts

A. 1. Andrew Jackson
   2. George Washington
   3. James Madison
   4. John Tyler
   5. Rutherford B. Hayes
   6. Thomas Jefferson
   7. Lyndon Johnson
   8. James Buchanan
   9. Harry Truman
   10. Richard Nixon
   11. Franklin Roosevelt
   12. Dwight Eisenhower
   13. Theodore Roosevelt
   14. Martin Van Buren
   15. John F. Kennedy
   16. James Monroe
   17. Calvin Coolidge

Q. Who was president when:

1 1. The Korean War began?
2. The Homestead Act was passed?
3. The Bill of Rights was added to the Constitution?
2 4. The Lewis and Clark expedition took place?
3 5. Japan surrendered at the end of World War II?
4 6. Texas was annexed by a joint resolution of Congress?
5 7. The Supreme Court ended segregation in the public schools?
6 8. The St. Lawrence Seaway was opened to shipping?
9. The Erie Canal was completed?
7 10. Gold was discovered in California in 1848?
11. The Treaty of Versailles was rejected by the U.S. Senate?
12. The Kansas-Nebraska Act was passed?
13. A civil service system was established?
14. The Second Bank of the U.S. was killed?
8 15. The Statue of Liberty was dedicated?
16. The Japanese bombed Pearl Harbor?
9 17. The Confederates fired on Fort Sumter in the harbor of Charleston, South Carolina?
18. John Marshall was appointed Chief Justice of the United States?
10 19. The Women's Suffrage Amendment (Article XIX) was ratified?
20. Alexander Hamilton presented his plan for funding the national debt?
11 21. The Tennessee Valley Authority was established?
22. The Haymarket Affair took place in Chicago?
23. The Income Tax Amendment (the 16th) was ratified?
24. The social security program was adopted?
12 25. The stock market crashed in 1929?
26. The United States obtained the Philippines, Guam, and Puerto Rico from Spain?

68

A. 1. Harry S. Truman (1950)
   2. Abraham Lincoln (1862)
   3. George Washington (1791)
   4. Thomas Jefferson (1804-06)
   5. Harry S. Truman (1945)
   6. John Tyler (1845)
   7. Dwight D. Eisenhower (1954)
   8. Dwight D. Eisenhower (1959)
   9. John Q. Adams (1825)
   10. James Polk
   11. Woodrow Wilson (1919 and 1920)
   12. Franklin Pierce (1854)
   13. Chester A. Arthur (1883)
   14. Andrew Jackson (1832)
   15. Grover Cleveland (1886)
   16. Franklin Roosevelt (1941)
   17. Abraham Lincoln (1861)
   18. John Adams (1801)
   19. Woodrow Wilson (1920)
   20. George Washington (1789-92)
   21. Franklin Roosevelt (1933)
   22. Grover Cleveland (1886)
   23. William H. Taft (February, 1913)
   24. Franklin Roosevelt (1935)
   25. Herbert Hoover
   26. William McKinley (1898)

Q. Who was president when:

27. Alaska was purchased from Russia?
28. The Gadsden Purchase was made from Mexico?
29. The first transcontinental railroad was completed?
30. An Independent Treasury was first established?
31. The last troops were removed from the reconstructed South?
32. The Berlin Airlift saved West Berlin?
33. The War of 1812 began?
34. The Supreme Court made its decision in the Dred Scott case?
35. The Cuban missile crisis occurred?
36. The United States declared war on Spain?
37. The Louisiana Purchase doubled the size of the U.S.?
38. The Virgin Islands were purchased from Denmark?
39. The Department of Health, Education, and Welfare was started?
40. The United States ended its first alliance with France?
41. The Teapot Dome Scandal occurred?
42. The American Federation of Labor was organized?
43. The First World War started?
44. The Mexican War took place?
45. The "Era of Good Feeling" occurred?
46. The 47th and 48th states (New Mexico and Arizona) were admitted to the Union?
47. Atomic bombs were dropped over Hiroshima and Nagasaki?
48. The first man landed on the moon?
49. The doctrine of judicial review was used in the case of *Marbury v. Madison*?
50. The Alien and Sedition Acts were passed?
51. The White House was burned by the British?
52. The boundary line between Maine and Canada was finally settled?

70

A. 27. Andrew Johnson (1867)
   28. Franklin Pierce (1854)
   29.Ulysses S. Grant (1869)
   30.Martin Van Buren (1840)
   31.Rutherford B. Hayes (1877)
   32.Harry S. Truman (1948-49)
   33.James Madison
   34.James Buchanan (1857)
   35.John F. Kennedy (1962)
   36.William McKinley (1898)
   37.Thomas Jefferson (1803)
   38.Woodrow Wilson (1916-17)
   39.Dwight Eisenhower (1953)
   40.John Adams (1800)
   41.Warren Harding
   42.Grover Cleveland (1886)
   43.Woodrow Wilson
   44.James Polk
   45.James Monroe
   46.William H. Taft
   47.Harry S. Truman
   48.Richard Nixon
   49.Thomas Jefferson
   50.John Adams (1798)
   51.James Madison
   52.John Tyler

Q. Certain mottos or catchwords have been associated with particular presidential administrations. With which president do you associate the following phrases?

1. The New Freedom
2. The Great Society
3. A Full Dinner Pail
4. Two Chickens in Every Pot
5. The Fair Deal
6. Big Stick Diplomacy
7. Dollar Diplomacy
8. The New Deal
9. The Square Deal
10. The New Frontier
11. Fifty-Four Forty or Fight
12. Tippecanoe and Tyler Too

A.

1. Woodrow Wilson
2. Lyndon B. Johnson
3. William McKinley
4. Herbert Hoover
5. Harry S. Truman
6. Theodore Roosevelt
7. William H. Taft
8. Franklin D. Roosevelt
9. Theodore Roosevelt
10. John F. Kennedy
11. James K. Polk
12. William H. Harrison

Presidential Nicknames

Q. Many of our presidents had nicknames. Who was

1. The Father of the Constitution
2. His Accidency
3. Teddy
4. The Tennessee Tailor
5. King Andrew the First
6. Napoleon of the Stamp
7. The Father of His Country
8. His Rotundity
9. The Sage of Monticello
10. Honest Abe
11. Silent Cal
12. Uncle Sam
13. The Rail Splitter
14. Old Hickory
15. Old Man Eloquent
16. Ike
17. That Man in the White House
18. Old Rough and Ready
19. Handsome Frank
20. Old Buck
21. The Little Magician of Kinderhook
22. The Man from Independence
23. His Fraudulency
24. The Hero of San Juan Hill

A.
1. James Madison
2. John Tyler
3. Theodore Roosevelt
4. Andrew Johnson
5. Andrew Jackson
6. James K. Polk
7. George Washington
8. John Adams
9. Thomas Jefferson
10. Abraham Lincoln
11 Calvin Coolidge
12 Ulysses S. Grant
13. Abraham Lincoln
14. Andrew Jackson
15. John Quincy Adams
16. Dwight D. Eisenhower
17. Franklin D. Roosevelt
18. Zachary Taylor
19. Franklin Pierce
20. James Buchanan
21. Martin Van Buren
22. Harry S. Truman
23. Rutherford B. Hayes
24. Theodore Roosevelt

Vice-Presidents

Q. Vice-presidents, especially those who never succeeded to the presidency, tend to be unknown by most Americans. Some of them deserve to be unknown, while others were distinguished politicians. Can you match the following vice-presidents with the president under whom they served?

1. Alben Barkley	A. Van Buren
2. Elbridge Gerry	B. Madison
3. Hannibal Hamlin	C. Jefferson
4. Levi Morton	D. Truman
5. George Clinton	E. Hoover
6. Charles Dawes	F. Wilson
7. Richard M. Johnson	G. Polk
8. Charles Fairbanks	H. Taft
9. Daniel Tompkins	I. McKinley
10. Thomas Marshall	J. Theodore Roosevelt
11. James S. Sherman	K. Coolidge
12. George M. Dallas	L. Lincoln
13. William Wheeler	M. Pierce
14. Garret Hobart	N. Benjamin Harrison

15. Henry Wilson	O. Grant (first term)
16. Schuyler Colfax	P. Grant (second term)
17. John Breckinridge	Q. Monroe
18. Charles Curtis	R. Cleveland (first term)
19. Thomas Hendricks	S. Buchanan
20. William R. King	T. Hayes

A.
1. D	5. C & B	9. Q	13. T	17. S
2. B	6. K	10. F	14. I	18. E
3. L	7. A	11. H	15. P	19. R
4. N	8. J	12. G	16. O	20. M

Events and Places Quiz

Q. What is the best source of information on the work of the Constitutional Convention of 1787?

A. The notes of James Madison, which were sold to the U.S. government and published in 1840 as the *Journal of the Federal Convention*. Madison kept excellent summaries of the debates during the convention but he made changes in some of these records in the last years of his life.

Q. What was the Congressional "hole in the wall" of the 1850s?

A. It was a counter just outside the door of the Senate and House where a member of Congress could get a highball. Roy F. Nichols tells how the custom was to eat a large breakfast and then not eat again until Congress adjourned in the late afternoon. The members of Congress lasted through this long period without food by stepping out to the "hole in the wall" for a nip. The result, said Nichols, was that very little in the *Congressional Globe* is accurate. The members would, however, fix up their remarks the next morning when they were sober.

Q. Was the Constitution drafted by a group of old men?

A. The average age of the fifty-five men who attended the Constitutional Convention in Philadelphia in 1787 was forty-two.

Q. When was the first American submarine used?

A. The *American Turtle* was invented by David Bushnell of Connecticut. In September, 1776, the Turtle, piloted by Sergeant Ezra Lee failed to fasten a bomb to an English ship, the *Eagle*, in New York harbor. Although the ship itself worked, the little submarine, which could operate under water for only a few minutes, was discarded.

Q. Did the Liberty Bell ring out liberty in Philadelphia on July 4, 1776?

A. No. The bell was not rung on July 4, 1776. It was rung on July 8, when the Declaration was proclaimed in Philadelphia. After peace came in 1783, the bell was called the "Independence Bell." It cracked in 1835 while ringing for

the funeral of Chief Justice John Marshall. The name "Liberty Bell" was used in 1839 in connection with the antislavery movement that was strong at that time. The bell was rung to celebrate the birth date of Washington in 1846 and it then cracked beyond repair.

Q. When was the first shift in power from one popular party to another, without a revolution or some sort of upheaval?

A. In 1801, when the Jeffersonian Republicans took over the national government from the Federalists.

Q. When did the U.S. Navy have its first mutiny?

A. In December, 1842, about twenty men on the U.S.S. *Somers* mutinied against their captain, Commander A. S. MacKenzie. The mutiny was supposedly led by Philip Spencer, whose father was Secretary of War. MacKenzie suppressed the mutiny, held trials aboard ship, and hanged Spencer and two others. MacKenzie himself was court-martialed when he returned home but was found not guilty.

Q. What is wrong with the painting of Washington crossing the Delaware painted by Emanuel Leutze in 1851?

A. The painting, besides showing Washington standing in an awkward position, displays a flag that was not approved by Congress until six months after the crossing. The painting was done in Germany and the river is the Rhine, not the Delaware. There was snow at the time but there is no record of the river being filled with ice.

Q. When did the United States become independent?

A. Richard Henry Lee's resolution for independence, a confederation, and foreign alliances was adopted by the Second Continental Congress on July 2, 1776. This action cut our ties with the British government. The Declaration, adopted two days later, merely justified the earlier action of the Congress.

Q. What was the first scandal about a Cabinet member?

A. Alexander Hamilton revealed in 1796 (after leaving the Cabinet) that he had been guilty of adultery with a Mrs. James Reynolds. Her husband had blackmailed Hamilton and was making further threats, so that Hamilton was forced to disclose the matter.

Q. Where did the idea of secession first develop?

A. Usually secession is associated with the South, and people like John Calhoun, from the 1830s on. Actually, the idea began in New England with groups like the Essex Junto during the administration of President Jefferson.

Q. What war was caused by an ear?

A. The war of Jenkins's Ear, which in this country was known as King George's War. Robert Jenkins, an English sea captain and smuggler, claimed to have lost an ear to the Spanish off the coast of Florida. When he displayed the severed object to Parliament in 1739, the Parliament, already angered with Spain, called for war. In America the war was named for King George II.

Q. Who named America?

A. Americus Vespucci, a Florentine merchant and banker, explored (in several expeditions) more than two-thirds of the eastern coastline of South America. A geographer, Martin Waldseemuller, proposed in 1507 that the newly discovered world be called the "land of Americus" for Americus, its discoverer. Poor Columbus lost out.

Q. What city has played host to the largest number of political conventions?

A. Chicago, Illinois — fourteen Republican and ten Democratic conventions since 1856.

Q. Who said "Nothing is certain but death and taxes"?

A. Benjamin Franklin.

Q. Do citizens get their right to vote from the Federal Constitution?

A. No. The right to vote is received from the states. The Constitution does say that in granting voting rights a state may not discriminate because of race, religion, sex, or age if the voter is over eighteen.

Q. In what year did the two major parties each hold their first convention?

A. In 1832. The Democrats nominated Andrew Jackson and the National Republicans nominated Henry Clay.

Q. In what city were the first conventions held?

A. In Baltimore, Maryland.

Q. Which president served the most years in the White House?

A. Franklin D. Roosevelt served twelve years.

Q. Who were the mugwumps?

A. The mugwumps were a faction of the Republican party who refused to support James G. Blaine and supported Grover Cleveland instead. Mugwump is an Algonquin word meaning "chief."

Q. What was the American Party or Know Nothing Party?

A. The American Party or Know Nothing Party was organized in 1854. The first national convention was held on June 5, 1855, in Philadelphia, Pennsylvania. The Party was originally a secret organization rather than a political party. Membership was divided into three classes: the first included members who were American born and were wholly unconnected with the Roman Catholic Church; they were obliged to vote as the Society determined. The second class included members who were permitted to hold office inside the organization. The third class was composed of members who were eligible to hold office outside the organization. On February 18, 1856, at a convention held in Philadelphia, the secret character of the organization was abolished. The convention then made presidential nominations: former President Millard Filmore of New York for president and Andrew Jackson Donaldson of Tennessee for vice-president. Filmore received only eight electoral votes. The name "American Party" was used by organizations in 1874 and 1887, but each was a distinct and separate party. George Wallace ran under the American Party name in 1968-72. The name, however, was all that was similar between the two parties.

Q. Who was the first Cabinet member who was a brother of a president?

A. Robert Francis Kennedy, who took office as the Attorney General in the Cabinet of President John F. Kennedy on January 21, 1961.

Q. Who wrote the song "America"?

A. Dr. Samuel Francis Smith, a Baptist Minister, wrote the song on a scrap of paper in half an hour. The song was first sung publicly on July 4, 1832, in the Parks Street Church in Boston, Massachusetts, by school children of Boston.

Q. Who was the president of the Confederate States of America?

A. Jefferson Davis of Mississippi was elected February 9, 1861. He was inducted into office, February 18, 1861, and delivered his inaugural address on the steps of the State Capitol at Montgomery, Alabama. Alexander Hamilton Stephens, of Georgia, was sworn in as vice-president on February 11, 1861. Much of the time Davis and Stephens were not on speaking terms.

Q. The grandson of the twenty-fourth vice-president ran for president twice but was defeated. What was his name?

A. Adlai Ewing Stevenson.

Q. Who was the first president of the First Continental Congress?

A. Peyton Randolph, a delegate from Virginia, was elected September 5, 1774, the day Congress was assembled. He resigned October 22, 1774, to attend the Virginia State Legislature, and his place was taken on the same day by Henry Middleton of South Carolina.

Q. Which presidents died in the White House?

A. While other presidents have died in office, William H. Harrison and Zachary Taylor are the only ones who died in the White House itself.

Q. Who was the first woman presidential candidate?

A. Victoria Woodhull, who was nominated by the Equal Rights Party in 1872.

Q. Who was the famous running mate of Victoria Woodhull, first woman presidential candidate?

A. Frederick Douglass, the black author and abolitionist.

Q. Women first voted nationwide in which presidential election?

A. In 1920, after the ratification of the Nineteenth Amendment.

Q. In Harriet Beecher Stowe's book, *Uncle Tom's Cabin*, was Uncle Tom really an "Uncle Tom"?

A. No. In the novel Uncle Tom was flogged to death because he refused to beat a female slave. His actions were just the opposite of the modern meaning of Uncle Tom.

Q. When did a chief justice of the United States preside over a meeting of the U. S. Senate?

A. In 1868, when Justice Samuel P. Chase presided over the impeachment trial of President Andrew Johnson. The Constitution provides that the Chief Justice preside at the trial of a president. In other impeachment proceedings, the president of the Senate presides.

Q. What was the Billion Dollar Congress?

A. In 1687, Congress for the first time passed a budget calling for expenditures of over one billion dollars.

Q. What was the Charter Oak?

A. In 1687 Governor Edward Andros, who was trying to force the northern colonies into a Dominion of New England, demanded that Connecticut give up her charter. During the discussions, so legend has it, the candles blew out, and when relit, the Charter was missing. It had been taken outside and hidden in an oak tree by Captain Joseph Wadsworth. Andros never got the charter but he put Connecticut into the Dominion. The oak tree died in 1856.

Q. When did the United States appoint its first ambassadors?

A. The U.S. appointed its first ambassadors in 1893. Believing that ambassadors were the personal representatives of kings, the country used the title of "Minister" for its highest ranking diplomats before 1893.

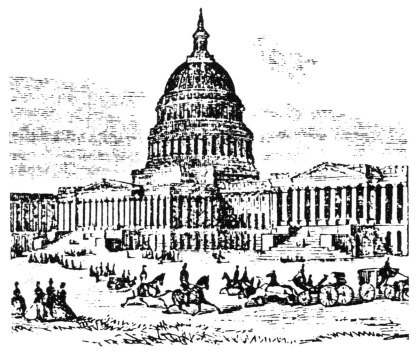

Q. In the first seventy years of this country's history, the Supreme Court acted on only two occasions to set aside laws passed by the Congress as unconstitutional. What were the occasions?

A. The first occurred in 1803 in the case of Marbury *v.* Madison. A section of the Judiciary Act of 1789 was set aside. In the Dred Scott case, 1857, the court nullified the Missouri compromise line, although the law had been repealed three years earlier.

Q. What were the names of the original thirteen states?

A. Connecticut   New York
Delaware   North Carolina
Georgia   Pennsylvania
Maryland   Rhode Island
Massachusetts   South Carolina
New Hampshire   Virginia
New Jersey

Q. Do the words "slave" or "slavery" appear in the U.S. Constitution?

A. No. Although several clauses in the Constitution really deal with slavery, the word is not used. Instead, the Constitution mentions "three-fifths of all other persons," or "no person held to service or labor in one State," or some other phrase that means slaves. The word "slavery" does appear in the Thirteenth Amendment which brought slavery to an end.

Q. How long was Jamestown the capital of Virginia?

A. Only during the seventeenth century. Jamestown was founded in 1607. In 1619 the first legislative assembly met in the church there. The town was burned in 1676 during Nathaniel Bacon's Rebellion and declined rapidly. After another fire in 1698 the Virginia government was moved to Williamsburg in 1699. Jamestown declined very rapidly and was soon a ghost town. Williamsburg was the capital until 1780 when it was moved to Richmond.

Q. Who said "War is hell"?

A. General William Tecumseh Sherman of Civil War fame is always associated with these words. Sherman, himself, could never remember saying them.

Q. When was corporal punishment ended in the U.S. Army?

A. Congress prohibited corporal punishment in the form of stripes or lashes in 1812. Military commanders thought this action by Congress hurt discipline. In 1833, whipping was restored for men who were convicted of desertion.

Q. A famous quotation to come of the Spanish-American War was "Carry a message to Garcia." Who was Garcia and who carried the message?

A. Garcia was the leader of the Cuban rebels in 1898. He was not within the reach of communications when the United States declared war against Spain. President McKinley wished to get in touch with the Cuban leader. Andrew Summers Rowan volunteered to take the message. In April, 1898, Rowan landed in Cuba and spent three weeks crossing the island. He found Garcia, delivered the message, and brought back a report on the rebels's military situation.

Q. Who were the Locofocos?

A. They were a group of radical Democrats who took control of a nomination convention in New York City in September, 1835. Their opponents (the minority) turned off the gas in the meeting hall, but the majority used new self-igniting matches called "Locofocos" to give light for the rest of the meeting. The name stuck to the radicals who opposed protective tariffs, paper money, banks, and corporations. By 1839, the Van Buren Democrats in New York accepted the Locofocos back into the regular Democratic party.

Q. Who held the first nominating convention for national office?

A. The Anti-Masonic Party held the first nominating convention on September 26, 1831, in Baltimore. This was also the first party to announce a platform. It was also the first important third party in our history.

Q. When did the U.S. Army stop the daily ration of liquor to the troops?

A. The daily ration as established in 1802 provided for a gill of rum, whisky, or brandy to be issued. In December, 1830, an order by the Adjutant General's Office ended the daily ration. For two years a sum of money was given in place of the whiskey ration, but even this was stopped in 1832.

Q. When did Congress give away a part of the District of Columbia?

A. In 1846,Congress ceded back to Virginia that part of the District south of the Potomac River. This region comprised about one-third of the District. The bill received little opposition in Congress or the press.

Q. Who said "An honest politician is one who when he is bought will stay bought"?

A. Long before Watergate, Simon Cameron (1799-1889), the U.S. Senator and political boss of Pennsylvania uttered these words. He served for nearly a year as Lincoln's first Secretary of War. Lincoln let him resign because the War Department's books were in bad shape.

Q. What is the only constitutional amendment that has been repealed?

A. The Nineteenth (providing for Prohibition) was ratified in 1919 and repealed by the Twenty-First Amendment in 1933.

Q. Where is the Mason-Dixon line?

A. The Mason-Dixon line is the boundary line between Pennsylvania and Maryland. Throughout the colonial period, this boundary was in dispute between the Penn family and the Calvert family. The line was surveyed by two English surveyors, Charles Mason and Jeremy Dixon, between 1763 and 1767. The Crown ratified the line in 1769.

Q. What is the oldest American settlement in Alaska?

A. Juneau. It was named for Joseph Juneau, who discovered the mineral riches of the area.

Q. After the Battle of the Little Big Horn, did any man or animal from Custer's command survive?

A. Commanche, the horse of Captain Meyers Keogh, Seventh Cavalry, was the only living creature left of Custer's old command.

Q. Was the Declaration of Independence signed on July 4, 1776?

A. Only by John Hancock, the President of Congress, and Charles Thomson, the Secretary of Congress. The parchment copy was not signed by the delegates until August 2, 1776. Some of the members of the Congress signed even later.

Q. What ships were involved in the Boston Tea Party?

A. The party took place on December 16, 1773. Between thirty and sixty men boarded three ships, the *Beaver*, the *Eleanor*, and the *Dartmouth*. They threw overboard 340 chests of tea.

Q. What state first ratified the Constitution?

A. The first state to ratify the Constitution was Delaware on December 7, 1787. It has been called the "First State" ever since.

Q. How did the Indians capture Fort Michilimackinac on June 2, 1763?

A. The French had built Fort Michilimackinac in 1700. The British had taken over the fort at the end of the French and Indian War. In 1763, the chief of the Chippewas, Minavavana, proposed to the commandant of the fort that the Indians stage a lacrosse-type game to celebrate King George's birthday on June 2. During the game, the ball was hit inside the fort. As the players ran to get the ball, they grabbed guns hidden beneath the blankets of their women. They killed twenty British soldiers and one trader, and took the rest of the garrison prisoners.

Q. What state has been under six flags?

A. Texas. These include the flags of Spain, France, Mexico, the Lone Star Republic of Texas, the Confederate States of America, and the United States.

Q. How many inventions did Thomas A. Edison invent?

A. Edison was probably the most prolific inventor in the nation's history. He obtained more than 1000 patents.

Q. Who were the Straight-Outs?

A. The Straight-Outs were a small group within the Democratic party who refused to support Horace Greeley as the Democratic candidate for president in 1872. The Straight-Outs met in Louisville, Kentucky, and nominated Charles O'Connor, a New York attorney, as their candidate.

Q. What is the meaning of pork-barrel?

A. The term "pork-barrel" refers to the practice of Congress in making government appropriations for local projects that are designed to please voters and help congressmen win re-election.

Q. What is the difference between a plurality of the vote and a majority of the vote?

A. Plurality refers to the number of votes the leading candidate received over his nearest rival. A majority vote means more than half the votes cast.

Q. Who said "We must indeed all hang together or most assuredly we shall all hang separately"?

A. This anecdote is attributed to Benjamin Franklin speaking to John Hancock as Congress prepared to sign the Declaration of Independence. There is no contemporary record of the story.

Q. Who was the last survivor of the *Mayflower*?

A. John Alden was twenty-one when he signed the Mayflower Compact in 1620. When he died in 1687, he was the last of those who came to Plymouth in that famous ship.

Q. What members of the Constitutional Convention never attended it?

A. Ten men were elected to the Convention but did not attend. The number included people like Patrick Henry, who refused to come, saying, "I smell a rat." Sixteen members of the Convention attended the proceedings but refused to sign the final document. A number of leaders of the revolutionary period were not present at the Convention. John Hancock was Governor of Massachusetts; John Adams was our minister to Great Britain; Thomas Jefferson was our minister to France; Samuel Adams and Richard Henry Lee were not chosen as delegates. Thirty-nine of the Convention delegates signed the Constitution.

Q. Do all revenue and appropriation bills originate in the federal House of Representatives?

A. The Constitution does provide (Article I, Section 7, Paragraph 1) that all revenue bills shall originate in the House of Representatives. The Senate may propose amendments to such bills.

Q. When did the First Congress of the United States actually begin to function?

A. Following the adoption of the Constitution, the First Congress should have begun on March 4, 1789. Some members of the House and the Senate were in New York on that day and took their seats, but neither house had a quorum, so they adjourned. They continued to meet daily but adjourned because they still lacked a quorum. The House of Representatives finally obtained a quorum on April 1, 1789, and proceeded to organize itself. The Senate did not obtain a quorum until April 6, 1789, and it then began its official business.

Q. What is the franking privilege?

A. Congress permits its members, certain other government officials, and once in a while a person whom it desires to honor, the privilege of sending through the mails unstamped letters and literature. For these public officials and members, this privilege applies only to their public correspondence and not their private correspondence.

Q. When was the Democratic party founded?

A. In 1824 all of the candidates for president belonged to the Republican Party, the party begun by Thomas Jefferson. As a result of the disputed election of John Quincy Adams to the presidency, the Republicans split into two groups. The Adams-Clay group became the National Republicans and in the 1830s were referred to as the Whigs. The followers of Andrew Jackson called themselves the Democratic-Republicans and later shortened their name to the Democratic Party. Thus today, the Democrats look to Jefferson and Jackson as the founders of their party.

Q. What American war had the highest casualty rate?

A. The Civil War brought the greatest loss of life of any of the wars that the United States has entered. The Union produced an official casualty list of 93,443 killed in action or dead of wounds and 210,400 dead of disease. Estimates of Confederate losses vary widely. It is probably safe to say that at least 540,000 Americans out of a population of thirty-one million lost their lives.

Q. What are some of the firsts concerning the Civil War?

A. According to the Civil War Centennial Commission, the Civil War was the first war in which:

- railroads were used extensively for moving supplies and troops rapidly from one theater to another.
- medical care was systematically organized.
- national conscription was used.
- national laws were passed so that soldiers and sailors could vote.
- rifled artillery came into general use.
- mobile railroad artillery was used.
- the repeating rifle was used by large units of troops.
- recognized news correspondents provided large-scale coverage at the front.
- wire entanglements were used in fortifying fields.
- the Medal of Honor was awarded.
- the electric telegraph was widely used to direct operations.
- aerial reconnaissance from anchored balloons was effectively used.
- a multi-manned submarine sank a surface vessel.
- ironclad ships opposed each other in battle.
- naval mines were widely used.
- a practical machine gun was developed.
- soldiers, equipment, and sites were extensively photographed.

Q. Who designed the White House?

A. The government sponsored a competition for a presidential mansion. James Hoban submitted the Georgian design that won. Hoban later directed the construction of the building. Congress voted a prize of either a gold medal or $500 for the competition. Hoban had a large family so he took the money. The term "White House" was not used until the building was whitewashed to cover the smoke marks following the British burning of the building in 1814.

Q. What was the Underground Railway?

A. The Underground Railway was a system for helping runaway slaves escape. Most of these slaves came from the upper South and were assisted to various routes across the free states. The stations were usually twenty or more miles apart. They were in the attics or cellars of private homes, in barns, or other places where the fugitives could sleep or eat during the day and be sent on their way at night.

Q. The Confederate battle flag of 1863 had thirteen stars although there were only eleven states that seceded. Why?

A. Kentucky and Missouri remained in the Union as far as the federal government was concerned, but these states had a large proportion of the population that was sympathetic to the Confederacy. Both states had representatives in the Confederate Congress and that is why there are thirteen stars in the 1863 flag.

Q. How long did it take to draft the Constitution of the United States?

A. One long, hot summer in Philadelphia in 1787. The fifty-five delegates at the Federal Convention worked well together. They began their meetings on May 25. By July 26, they had dropped the idea of amending the Articles of Confederation (their original charge) and instead had adopted the framework for the Constitution. The Committee of Detail worked on the version during most of August. The sharpest conflicts of the Convention had to do with designing the office of president. By September 12, the Committee of Style presented to the delegates the final version of the Constitution. On September 17, 1787, the Convention sent the Constitution to the Continental Congress to be transmitted to the states.

Q. What was the first Confederate state to be readmitted to the Union after the Civil War?

A. Tennessee, in July, 1866.

Q. What trade did Paul Revere practice?

A. Besides being a goldsmith and silversmith, Revere was also an engraver and a dentist. He also cast iron and brass and owned a copper-rolling mill.

Q. How many states were there in the Union at the close of the War of 1812?

A. There were eighteen states in the Union when the war was ended by the Treaty of Ghent in December, 1814. The news of the treaty did not reach the United States until after General Andrew Jackson had won the Battle of New Orleans in January, 1815.

Q. Who was the first president of the Republic of Texas?

A. Sam Houston was elected president on September 5, 1836. He was sworn in on October 22, 1836. After Texas became a state in December, 1845, Houston served in the U.S. Senate from 1846 to 1859. He then became Governor of Texas. He was deposed as governor in 1861 when he refused to support secession.

Q. What state was a quasi-independent republic for fourteen years before joining the Union?

A. Vermont claimed to be a republic from 1777 until its admission to the Union in 1791.

107

Q. Where did the Continental Congress meet?

A. The Continental Congress met in eight different places. The First Continental Congress met in Philadelphia in 1774. The Second Continental Congress also first met in Philadelphia, but because of military and political events, the Congress also met in New York City, Princeton, Trenton, Reading, York, Baltimore, and Annapolis.

Q. What were the names of the ships that brought the first colonists to Jamestown, Virginia?

A. Three ships, the *Discovery*, the *Godspeed*, and the *Susan Constant*, sailed from England in December, 1606, with 144 colonists. The ships arrived off the Virginia coast in April, 1607. After searching a month for a landing site, the colonists chose a piece of land jutting into the James River, some thirty miles from the sea. The spot was low and marshy and a poor place for a new settlement.

Q. How many guns constitute a national salute?

A. Twenty-one guns are the national salute and are also the salute to a national flag. A twenty-one gun salute is also rendered to the president of the United States, to an ex-president, and to a president-elect.

Q. Was the U.S. flag ever flown during a battle in the Revolutionary War?

A. No. The flag was approved by the Second Continental Congress on June 14, 1777. Although some paintings show the flag being flown during a battle, there is no evidence that this ever took place. Revolutionary troops carried state and other flags, but not the national emblem.

Personality Quiz

Q. Who invented the zipper?

A. The term "zipper" was first used for a hookless fastener for overshoes invented by Whitcomb L. Judson of Chicago about 1893. Gideon Sundback later improved a hookless fastener with patents obtained from 1913 to 1917. These patents were used by the manufacturers of the Talon Slide Fastener.

Q. Which twice-defeated presidential candidate was appointed U.S. Representative to the United Nations by President Kennedy?

A. Adlai Stevenson.

Q. Who invented the machine gun?

A. Richard J. Gatling. At the beginning of the Civil War, Gatling, although born in North Carolina, favored the North. He saw that a rapid-fire gun would be of great value to the Union cause. He received a patent for his weapon in November, 1862.

Q. Who invented the reaper or threshing machine?

A. Cyrus Hall McCormick, in 1832. McCormick's father had spent twenty years trying to invent a reaping machine, but it took the genius of the son to finally succeed. Although Cyrus McCormick had crude models in 1832, he did not set up his factory in Chicago until after the Panic of 1837.

Q. Who invented the Polaroid camera?

A. Edwin H. Land, in 1947. Land believed that his invention improved the art of photography by producing a finished photograph immediately after making the exposure.

Q. Who was the youngest man ever nominated for the presidency?

A. William Jennings Bryan, who was only thirty-six (in 1896).

Q. Who invented the cotton gin?

A. Eli Whitney in 1793. While visiting a plantation in Georgia, Whitney saw the slaves slowly removing seeds from the cotton bolls. In about ten days he devised a system to speed up the process. A cylinder with tiny hooks pulled the cotton fiber through narrow slots, removing the seeds. A second cylinder covered with brushes cleaned the cotton off the hooks. Whitney is frequently referred to as the inventor of the system of interchangeable parts. He did not invent the system but was the first to use it on a wide scale.

Q. What president's wife was once United States representative to the United Nations?

A. Eleanor Roosevelt, wife of Franklin.

Q. Who was Arizona's only presidential candidate?

A. Barry Goldwater.

Q. What was the first state admitted to the Union after the ratification of the Constitution by the original thirteen colonies?

A. Vermont, on March 4, 1791.

Q. What Ohio Governor was crushed in the 1920 presidential election?

A. James Cox.

Q. Who invented toothpaste tubes?

A. A Connecticut dentist, Dr. Washington W. Sheffield, in 1892. Looking for a more sanitary way of keeping toothpastes than in jars, Sheffield struck on metal tubes. He began their production and soon Colgate was producing large numbers of tubes.

Q. Who invented the parking meter?

A. The credit goes to Carl C. Magee who developed the meter in 1935. Magee wanted to discover a system that would permit cities to charge for curb-parking. Oklahoma City, Oklahoma, adopted Magee's system in 1935 and the use of meters spread throughout the nation.

Q. Who was the first American woman to serve in the British Parliament?

A. Lady Nancy Langhorne Astor succeeded her husband in the House of Commons in 1919 when he became a member of the House of Lords. She was born in Greenwood, Virginia, in 1879.

Q. Who invented the Kodak camera?

A. George Eastman of Rochester, New York, registered the name "Kodak" in 1888 and began to sell a camera that he had patented four years earlier. Supposedly he used "K" which was the first letter of his mother's maiden name and then worked out a name that could easily be identified. The original camera had no finder, required no focusing, and had only one speed.

Q. Who was the inventor of toilet paper?
A. Joseph C. Gayetty of New York City, in 1857.

Q. What state has a unicameral legislature?
A. Nebraska, since 1934.

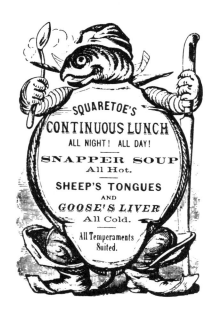

Q. Who invented the long-playing record?
A. Peter Goldmark produced the first LP record for Columbia Records in 1948.

Q. After the discovery of the North Pole, how long was it before the South Pole was reached?
A. About two years. Admiral Robert E. Perry reached the North Pole in April, 1909. Captain Roald Amundsen, a Norwegian, reached the South Pole in December, 1911.

Q. Where was Knute Rockne born and where was he educated?

A. Rockne was born in Voss, Norway. He was brought to this country at the age of three. His family settled in Chicago. Rockne received his B.S. from Notre Dame in 1914 and spent the rest of his career at that institution. He was assistant coach for football for four years, and head coach from 1918 until his death in 1931.

Q. Who was Eric Weiss?

A. The son of a rabbi, Eric Weiss took the stage name of Harry Houdini. When he was only eight, Houdini went on stage as a trapeze performer but he soon switched to magic.

Q. How many times was Mary Baker Eddy married?

A. The discoverer of Christian Science was married three times. Her first husband, George Washington Glover, died in 1844. In 1853 she married Daniel Patterson whom she divorced in 1873. She married Asa Gilbert Eddy in 1877 and he died in 1882.

Q. How did Wild Bill Hickock die?

A. Wild Bill was shot during a card game in Deadwood, South Dakota, on August 2, 1876.

Q. Did Calamity Jane really exist?

A. Yes. Calamity Jane was born Jane Burke in Princeton, Missouri, in 1852. She worked as an Indian scout and an aide to General Custer and General Miles. She also served as a government mail-carrier between Custer, Montana, and Deadwood South Dakota for a number of years. Calamity Jane died August 1, 1903 in Deadwood, South Dakota.

Q. Is there a second famous Benedict Arnold in American history besides the one known as a traitor during the Revolutionary War?

A. Yes. Benedict Arnold was the first governor of Rhode Island under the royal charter. He served as governor three times between the years 1663 and 1678.

Q. How long had Susan B. Anthony been prominent in the Women's Rights Movement before she attempted to cast a vote?

A. Susan B. Anthony had become a leader in the drive for Women's Rights in 1848. It was 1872 before she attempted to make a test case by trying to vote at the polls. She was arrested for her action.

Q. Who was the first man to discharge an explosive by means of an electrical charge sent over a wire?

A. As you might well expect, it was Benjamin Franklin. He also killed a turkey by this means and had it served at a banquet.

Q. Who was the first woman to obtain a medical degree in the United States?

A. Elizabeth Blackwell, who graduated from Geneva Medical College in 1849. She and her sister, Emily, started an Infirmary for Women and Children in New York in 1853, the first institution of its kind conducted solely by women. She was afterward connected with other forward steps in medical education both here and in England.

Q. Where and when was Clarence S. Darrow, the criminal lawyer, born and where was he educated?

A. Clarence Darrow was born in Kinsman, Ohio, in 1857. He was educated in the Ohio public schools, and gained his legal education largely by working and reading law in various lawyers offices. He was defense counsel in the Loeb-Leopold murder trial and in the Scopes trial concerning evolution. He also defended the blacks in the Scottsboro case. Darrow died in 1938.

Q. What eloquent Illinois governor was twice defeated for president by General Eisenhower?

A. Adlai Stevenson.

Q. What general, nicknamed "The Superb," lost the 1880 election to Garfield?

A. Winfield S. Hancock.

Q. Who was the first woman to be elected to the U.S. House of Representatives?

A. Jeanette Rankin of Montana, elected in 1916, took her seat in 1917.

Q. Who was John Fitch?

A. John Fitch was the inventor of the steamboat. In 1786 he built a boat shaped something like a canoe and operated it with steam-driven paddles on the Delaware River. He built a series of boats, one of which had side-paddle wheels. Unable to get enough financial backing, Fitch's ventures failed. Robert Fulton had greater success in securing money and his steamboat became a success.

Q. Which cartoonist originated the Democratic donkey and the Republican elephant?
A. Thomas Nast.

Q. Who was the Republican orator, known as the Great Agnostic, who nominated James G. Blaine for president in 1876, calling him "The Plumed Knight"?
A. Robert G. Ingersoll.

Q. Who was South Dakota's only presidential candidate?
A. George McGovern.

Q. What did the State of Texas do to Sam Houston at the beginning of the Civil War?
A. Sam Houston was Governor of Texas at the time. The state passed a law requiring him to take an oath of allegiance to the Confederacy. Houston, a Unionist, refused, and was deposed as governor. He died two years later.

Q. How did "Czar" Reed define a statesman?

A. Thomas B. Reed of Maine, Speaker of the House in much of the 1890s, described a statesman as "a successful politician who is dead."

Q. Who was the first woman to serve in the U.S. Senate?

A. Rebecca L. Felton of Georgia. She was appointed to the Senate by the Governor of Georgia in 1922, but served only two days after taking her oath, before being replaced by her elected successor.

Q. Though defeated by F.D.R. in 1940, this man was sent on a fact-finding trip around the world by the president. Who was he?

A. Wendell Wilkie.

Q. Who holds the record for being Speaker of the House of Representatives for the longest time?

A. Sam Rayburn of Texas. Rayburn was Speaker from 1940 to 1947; 1949 to 1953; and from 1955 to 1961 — some seventeen years.

Q. Who was the first American woman to demand the right to vote?

A. Probably Margaret Brent, in 1648. She lived in Maryland and was the first woman in that colony to own land in her own name. She helped Governor Leonard Calvert and he made her his executrix. In 1648, she asked to be made a member of the Maryland Assembly with the right to vote. Her request was refused. Angered, she moved to Virginia.

Q. Though defeated by Woodrow Wilson in 1916, this man twice served with distinction on the Supreme Court. Who was he?

A. Charles Evans Hughes.

Q. Who was the Republican Party's first presidential candidate?

A. John C. Fremont, the "Pathfinder," in 1856.

Q. One member of Congress voted against declaring war in both World War I and World War II. Who was this person?

A. Jeanette Rankin, a member of the House from Montana. She opposed both wars and voted against them.

Q. Who was the first black to have a seat in the House of Representatives?

A. Joseph H. Rainey, who was elected as a representative from South Carolina, and served from 1870 to 1879.

Q. Who was the first woman admitted to practice before the U.S. Supreme Court?

A. Belva Ann Bennett Lockwood, who lobbied for a law that would permit women lawyers to appear before the court. After the law was passed, she was admitted to practice before the court in 1879.

Q. What U.S. congressman was excluded from his seat in the House of Representatives, only to have the Supreme Court rule that such exclusion was unconstitutional?

A. Adam Clayton Powell, 1967. He was eventually seated by the House after the court ruling.

Q. Who was the New York colonial governor who was hanged?

A. Jacob Leisler, a New York merchant, learned of the ouster of King James II, and led his own revolt against the Dominion of New England government that had been imposed on New York. Leisler believed that the Dominion government was engaged in a plot to impose Catholicism. He was supported by people of various economic classes in New York in 1689. And although Leisler proclaimed William and Mary as the new monarchs, a Royal Governor came over from England, charged Leisler with treason, and had him hanged. Parliament later reversed the guilty verdict and restored the confiscated property of the dead governor to his family.

Q. Who was the first black woman to become a physician?

A. Susan Smith McKinney. She graduated from the New York Medical College in 1870, and, after postgraduate work, Dr. McKinney practiced in New York City and later in Ohio.

Q. What presidential candidate, who polled only 62,300 votes in the election of 1844, changed the result of the election?

A. James G. Birney, the Liberty party candidate. In New York, the crucial state, Birney received 15,812 votes, while Henry Clay had 232,482, and James Polk had 237,588 votes. If one-third of the Birney votes had gone to Clay, he would have carried New York, and would have become president.

Q. Who was the first black man to have his picture on a U.S. postage stamp?

A. Booker T. Washington's picture was placed on a 10¢ stamp (in the Famous American Series) in 1940.

Q. Who was Brother Jonathan?

A. Jonathan Turnbull as Governor of Connecticut had the confidence of George Washington. In times of difficulty, Washington was reported to have said, "I must consult Brother Jonathan." In the late 19th century, the term "Brother Jonathan" was used to designate an American.

Q. Who was the first black man to become a general in the U.S. Army?

A. Benjamin O. Davis, Sr. was promoted to the rank of Brigadier General in 1940. His son, Benjamin O. Davis, Jr. was the first black to become a general in the Air Force.

Q. Who was Lt. Charles Wilkes?

A. Wilkes, a lieutenant in the U.S. Navy, led a four-year expedition to the Antarctic and the South Seas. The expedition reached the Antarctic in January, 1841, and in February, landed on a part of the continent. These were the first Americans to reach the southernmost part of the world.

Q. Who was the first Jew to be elected to a public office?

A. Probably Frances Salvador, a plantation owner, who served in the South Carolina Provincial Congress. Salvador was killed in fighting in July, 1776, and was the first Jew to die in the Revolutionary War.

Q. How did the paper money issue affect a child's name?

A. "General" Jacob Coxey, who led the first march of unemployed workers from Ohio to Washington in 1894, was a great advocate of paper money. He hoped to encourage the government to issue paper money to help the unemployed. He named his son "Legal Tender Coxey."

Q. Who organized the first women's rights convention in the United States?

A. Elizabeth Cady Stanton and Lucretia C. Mott. The convention met in Seneca Falls, New York, in 1848.

Q. Did John C. Calhoun invent the idea of nullification?

A. No. James Madison and Thomas Jefferson, while opposing the Alien and Sedition Acts in 1798, wrote (separately) the Virginia and Kentucky Resolutions which contained the idea of nullification. They used the idea to defend liberty; Calhoun used it to defend slavery.

Q. Who was the founder and long-time president of the American Federation of Labor?

A. Samuel Gompers, an English immigrant, who, with the help of Adolph Strasser, set up an organization of national craft unions in 1886. Gompers headed the Cigarmakers Union at that time.

Q. Samuel F. B. Morse is known as the inventor of the telegraph. What other claim to fame did he have?

A. Morse was one of the best nineteenth century American artists. He was never financially successful as a painter, but he did make a small fortune from the telegraph.

Q. Who was the "Financier of the Revolution"?

A. Robert Morris, one of the richest men of his time, has been called the "Financier of the Revolution." A Philadelphia businessman who served in the Continental Congress, he was the first Superintendent of Finance. He spent several years in a debtor's prison in later life.

Q. Who served in the U.S. Senate for the longest time?

A. Senator Carl Hayden of Arizona. He served over forty-one years — from March, 1927 to May, 1968. He also served fifteen years in the House of Representatives.

Q. What happened to James Otis?

A. Otis, one of the leading patriots in Massachusetts in the 1760s, was attacked by a British customs official and severely beaten in 1769. He had a history of mental illnesses after this attack. The fiery patriot was finally killed by a bolt of lightning in 1783.

Q. Who was the first signer of the Declaration of Independence to die?

A. Button Gwinnett of Georgia. He died in May, 1777, of wounds received in a duel with General Lachlan McIntosh. Gwinnett's autograph is very rare.

Q. What American politician and diplomat had a flower named for him?

A. Joel Roberts Poinsett, who was our first Minister to Mexico (1825-29). He developed the plant known as the poinsettia.

Q. Who held the office of Secretary of State and Chief Justice of the United States at the same time?

A. John Marshall. He was Secretary of State in 1801 when John Adams nominated him as Chief Justice. Although confirmed in his new post, he continued to function as Secretary of State for the last two months of Adams's term.

Q. Who was the Speaker of the House of Representatives whose daughter was a famous actress?

A. William B. Bankhead, Speaker of the House in the 1930s. His daughter was Tallulah Bankhead.

132

Q. Who administered the presidential oath to George Washington at his first inauguration in New York in 1789?

A. Robert R. Livingston, the Chancellor of the State of New York, gave the oath on a balcony of the new Federal Building overlooking Wall Street.

Q. What is the Logan Act?

A. In 1798, relations between the U.S. and France were bad. The two countries were engaged in an undeclared war in the Caribbean. George Logan, a Philadelphia Quaker, decided to take direct steps to end the movement toward war. He sailed to France and carried on private negotiations with French officials in order to improve relations. Congress, upon learning of his actions, passed the Logan Act (1799) which prohibited private individuals from carrying on diplomatic negotiations with foreign governments on matters in dispute with the U.S.

Q. Who really deserves the title of "Father of Our Country"?

A. George Washington had no children. Perhaps the title should go to Sir William Johnson, the British Indian agent in the northern colonies. Sir William, who was adopted into the Iroquois tribes, was rumored in London to have fathered between 300 and 700 children.

Q. Only one American citizen who was not a member of the Senate has been voted the privileges of the Senate floor. Who was he?

A. The historian, George Bancroft, was granted this honor in 1879. When Bancroft died in 1891, there was national mourning in Washington and in all the cities through which his body passed on the way to burial in Massachusetts. Present at his funeral were the president, vice-president, and chief justice.

134

Q. Congress has granted honorary United States citizenship to two persons. Who were they?

A. The Marquis de Lafayette and Winston Churchill.

Q. What did Charles Lindbergh's father do?

A. Charles Augustus Lindbergh, Sr. was a lawyer and farmer in Minnesota who entered politics. He served in the U.S. House of Representatives from 1907 to 1917.

Q. What member of the Michigan legislature was also a king?

A. "King" James Strang of Beaver Island in Lake Michigan. After the death of Joseph Smith in Navoo, Illinois, Strang led a small group of Mormons into Wisconsin. In the late 1840s these people moved to the Beaver Islands. Strang was soon crowned as King James. He was elected to the state legislature in 1852 and was assassinated in 1856.

Q. What New York City mayor endeared himself to his constituents by reading the Sunday comics over the radio to the children of the city?

A. Fiorello H. LaGuardia, Mayor of New York, 1934-1945.

Q. Who produced the famous radio version of H.G. Wells's, War of the Worlds?

A. Orson Welles, on October 30, 1938. Although the program was interrupted with assurances that it was only fictional, many easterners panicked thinking that Martians were landing in New Jersey.

Q. Who led the formation of the Congress of Industrial Organizations (CIO)?

A. John L. Lewis of the United Mine Workers helped to set up the organization within the American Federation of Labor in 1935. Lewis favored the industry-wide union rather than the craft union. In 1936 when the AFL ordered an end to the movement, the CIO broke away and became an independent labor organization.

Q. Who was the Boy General?

A. George Armstrong Custer was often called the Boy General. He was twenty-four and only two years out of West Point when he was appointed a brigadier general in the Union Army.

Q. What vice-president and senator was expelled from the Senate, declared a traitor by the Senate, and forced to flee the country?

A. John Cakell Breckenridge of Kentucky, Vice-President under Buchanan, later served in the Senate. He was expelled in April, 1861, and declared a traitor in December, 1861. He fled his home state when it supported the Union cause and served as a major general in the Confederate Army. He served for a month or so as Secretary of State of the Confederacy (1865). After the war, he fled the country and went to Europe and Canada. The government allowed him to return to Kentucky in 1869.

Q. Who was the "Father of the United States Navy"?

A. Commodore John Barry, an Irishman, who was commissioned by the Continental Congress as its first naval commander.

136

Q. What were Beecher's Bibles?

A. The Rev. Henry Ward Beecher, a staunch anti-slavery man, encouraged easterners to send rifles to Kansas in the 1850s to prevent Kansas from being admitted as a pro-slavery state.

Q. What famous novelist ran for Governor of California on the Democratic ticket in 1934?

A. Upton Sinclair, author of *The Jungle* (1906). Sinclair surprised people by winning the primary, and he was only narrowly defeated in the general election. Starting in 1940, he published the long series of Lanny Budd novels.

Q. Who were the Hessian Flies?

A. Farmers during the Revolutionary War were constantly irritated by the foraging efforts of King George's German soldiers. The patriots called these soldiers "Hessian Flies."

Q. What famous historian was once Secretary of the Navy and later Minister to Great Britain?

A. George Bancroft, author of the first scholarly history of the U.S. (in ten volumes, 1834-74), was Secretary of the Navy from 1845 to 1846. He issued the order to the navy to take California and set up the Naval Academy at Annapolis.

Q. What statesman engaged in grape-juice diplomacy?

A. William Jennings Bryan, who served as Secretary of State from 1913 to 1915, was a strong supporter of the temperance movement. He served only grape juice at state functions, and thus his efforts were referred to as grape juice diplomacy.

Q. Who was the apostle to the Indians?

A. John Eliot, a seventeenth century Massachusetts clergyman, received his title for his missionary work among the Indians. In the 1660s he translated both the Old and New Testaments into Indian tongues.

Q. Who gave his name to an unfair method of redistricting election districts?

A. Elbridge Gerry who became vice-president in Madison's second term. He was governor of Massachusetts when a county had new election districts drawn up for it. The new district looked like a salamander and the name "gerry-mander" was coined.

Q. Who was the first American to write a tragedy that was acted on the professional stage?

A Thomas Godfrey of Philadelphia, who wrote *The Prince of Parthia* (1765).

Q. Who was the first American to make a profession out of writing novels?

A. Charles Brockden Brown was the first native-born author to have novel-writing as a profession. Brown began writing novels in 1798.

Q. Who was the Fighting Quaker?

A. General Nathanael Green was dropped from membership in the Quaker Church after he joined the army during the Revolutionary War. Greene was one of the finest generals in Washington's army.

Q. Which one of Washington's generals, during the Revolutionary War, claimed to have a title?

A. William Alexander, who fought at Long Island and was captured and also fought at Trenton and Brandywine. He claimed to be heir to the title of Earl of Stirling. Washington and his associates called Alexander Lord Stirling but the British never recognized his claims.

Q. Who killed Tecumseh in the Battle of the Thames?

A. Richard M. Johnson supposedly killed Tecumseh. Johnson was chosen as vice-president by the Senate in 1837.

Q. Who had as his slogan "Peace, it's wonderful"?

A. The Black evangelist of the 1930s and 1940s, Father Divine. He set up "Heavens" across the country and provided his followers with a common sharing of funds, plenty of food, and resort hotels.

Q. Who was the first black to serve a full term in the U.S. Senate?

A. Blanche Kelso Bruce of Mississippi. Born a slave in Virginia, Bruce was educated at Oberlin College, became a teacher and a planter in Mississippi. He served in the U.S. Senate from 1875-81.

Q. Who wrote, "Tyranny, like hell, is not easily conquered"?

A. Thomas Paine in 1776, in *The American Crisis*.

Q. What famous inventor's son was a member of the Cabinet?

A. Charles Edison, served as Secretary of the Navy from 1939 to 1940. He resigned to run for governor of New Jersey and won election to that post, 1940 to 1944.

Q. Who was the first woman to hold a Cabinet post?

A. Frances Perkins, who was appointed Secretary of Labor by President Franklin Roosevelt. She served in that office from 1933 to 1945.

Q. What Cabinet member was a relative of Napoleon Bonaparte?

A. Charles Joseph Bonaparte, Secretary of the Navy from 1905-06, and as Attorney General, 1906-09, was the grandson of Napoleon's brother, Jerome.

Q. Who was the author of "Dixie"?

A. A northerner, Daniel Emmett, from Mount Vernon, Ohio.

Q. Who was the first American, not American Indian, to be cremated?

A. Henry Laurens, the revolutionary patriot of South Carolina. Laurens had a fear that he might be buried while still alive. When he died in December, 1792, he ordered that his body be burned. His son carried out his wishes.

Q. Who discovered the source of the Mississippi River?

A. A lot of men thought that they had discovered the source of the "Father of Waters" but it was Henry Rowe Schoolcraft (1793-1864) who really succeeded. Schoolcraft had gone on an expedition with Lewis Cass in 1820, looking for the source of the Mississippi. But it was not until 1832 that Schoolcraft led an expedition that reached Lake Itasca in Minnesota.

Q. Who wrote "Rudolph the Red-Nosed Reindeer"?

A. Robert L. May, who was in the advertising department of Montgomery Ward's. In 1939 the mail-order company gave away 2.4 million copies of the story. In 1949 the story was set to music by Johnny Marks. Over 79 million records have been sold.

Q. What kind of legal training did John Marshall have?

A. Chief Justice John Marshall had six weeks of legal training at the College of William and Mary. He was then admitted to the Virginia Bar. His decisions are among the best of any justice of the nation's highest court.

Q. What did John D. Rockefeller do before he got into the oil business?

A. Rockefeller was a produce merchant who also dealt in meats and grain in Cleveland, Ohio. By the time he was twenty, Rockefeller and his partner had made a small fortune before oil attracted his attention.

Q. Who was the London-based European correspondent of the New York Tribune in the 1850s?

A. In the 1850s, the editor of the Tribune was Horace Greeley, and the managing editor, Charles A. Dana. Dana hired Karl Marx to write on European matters. From 1851 to 1862, Marx contributed about 500 articles and editorials. The money he received helped to keep his family from starving.

Q. Who developed central heating for American buildings?

A. Solomon Willard of Massachusetts developed a system of central heating in the 1820s. He drew up a plan calling for a basement furnace and pipes to conduct hot air to the various parts of the building. Willard also designed and built the monument to the Battle of Bunker Hill.

Q. Who was the Radio Priest?

A. Father Charles E. Coughlin, of the Shrine of the Little Flower in Royal Oak, Michigan. His Sunday afternoon programs in the 1930s were so popular that he received about 80,000 letters each week. He became involved in politics and at first was a staunch supporter of President Franklin Roosevelt. He turned against Roosevelt by 1934 when the President opposed some of Coughlin's inflationary proposals. He later became known as an anti-Semite and as a supporter of Hitler. He was finally silenced by his archbishop.

Q. Who developed the modern folding cardboard box?

A. In 1879, Robert Gair of New York had a factory in which he made paper bags. He developed a machine that made a folding paper carton.

Q. Who was George B. Shelden?

A. Shelden, of Rochester, New York, was the inventor of a "road engine" that ran on oil. He applied for a patent in 1878 but the patent was not granted until 1895. For a time Shelden collected a royalty on every automobile made in the United States. Shelden's patent was finally challenged by Henry Ford. The court upheld Shelden's patent in 1911 (just as the patent was about to expire) but said it did not apply to the type of engine that Ford was producing. Shelden won a moral victory but ceased to collect royalties.

Q. What pair of brothers played important roles in nineteenth century naval history?

A. Captain Oliver H. Perry (1784-1819) was the hero of the Battle of Lake Erie, (1813) during the War of 1812. His younger brother, Commodore Matthew C. Perry, (1794-1858) was responsible for opening Japan to western influence, 1853-54.

Q. Who was His Imperial Highness, Norton I, Emperor of the United States and Protector of Mexico?

A. Joshua A. Norton, an Englishman who lived in many parts of the world, went to San Francisco in 1849. He made and lost a fortune. In September, 1858, he proclaimed himself Emperor of the United States. He soon issued proclamations abolishing Congress and then the American republic. He dressed in fancy uniforms and was tolerated with kindness by the people of San Francisco. He rode the street cars, attended the theater, and ate in the best restaurants... all for free. In 1869 he suggested the idea of a Golden Gate bridge. When he died in 1880, ten-thousand people attended his funeral.

145

Q. Who said "The public be damned"?

A. Probably a lot of people. But the man who gets the credit is William Henry Vanderbilt, the president of New York Central Railroad. He made this remark in response to a reporter's question in Chicago in 1883.

Q. What kind of publicity did the Wright brothers get for their first flight?

A. Almost none. Although the first flight (of twelve seconds) was made on December 17, 1903, and many more were made in the following years, it was not until May, 1908, that reporters began to awaken the country to the magnificent accomplishment of the Wright brothers.

Q. Who started "Harolds Club" in Reno?

A. Raymond Smith, in the 1930s. He began the publicity that made Nevada gambling so popular. Smith named the club for his son but dropped the apostrophe.

Q. Who was John Philip Holland?

A. Holland is an unsung hero who finally brought the submarine to a state of practical value. Born in Ireland in 1840, Holland studied the works of earlier efforts to make a submarine. He emigrated to the United States in 1873 and hoped to get financing for his plans. He believed that a submarine could be used against the British navy to help bring about Irish independence. In 1881, using money from an Irish society (the Fenians), he built a three-man submarine. The *Fenian Ram* was launched in the Hudson River in May 1881, and made many successful runs. It embodied all of the principles used by modern submarines. After 1898, Holland built submarines for many nations.

Q. Who was William Plumer of New Hampshire?

A. Besides being Governor of New Hampshire, Plumer was the only elector to cast a vote against President James Monroe in the election of 1820. Legend has it that Plumer voted against Monroe because he "did not want Washington to be robbed of the glory of being the only president who had ever received the unanimous vote of the electors." There is no basis for this story. William Plumer voted against Monroe because he did not approve of Monroe's administration. Instead, he voted for John Quincy Adams whom he thought would be a better president than Monroe.

147

Miscellaneous Trivia Quiz

Q. When did the "Star Spangled Banner" become the national anthem of the United States?

A. It was not designated the national anthem until 1916, and was not confirmed by Congress until 1931. The words were inspired by U.S. valor under British bombardment at Fort McHenry in the War of 1812, but the music, ironically, is from a British song, "To Anacreon in Heaven."

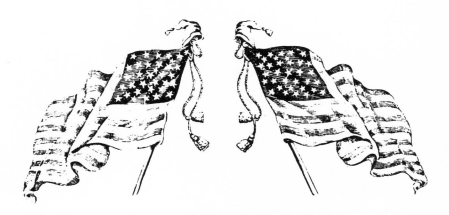

Q. How long would it take to spend one billion dollars?

A. If you had spent $1,000 a day every day since Christ was born, you would not as yet have spent one billion dollars.

Q. "My country! In her intercourse with foreign nations may she ever be right; but, right or wrong, my country!" Who said it?

A. Stephen Decatur, the naval hero of the war against the Barbary pirates, gave this toast at a dinner in Norfolk, Virginia, in April, 1816.

Q. Who invented the vacuum cleaner?

A. The first motor-driven machine was patented by John S. Thurman of St. Louis, in 1899.

Q. Who wrote, "We have met the enemy, and they are ours — two ships, two brigs, one schooner, and one sloop"?

A. These words were written by twenty-seven-year-old Lieutenant Oliver Hazard Perry on September 10, 1813. Perry had just defeated the British fleet in the Battle of Put-In-Bay in Lake Erie. He sent the message to the American military commander of the Northwest Territory, Major General William Henry Harrison.

Q. What happened to the bones of Thomas Paine?

A. The author of *Common Sense* died on June 8, 1809, and was buried at New Rochelle, New York. Because of his radical religious and political views, as well as his drinking problem, few friends showed up for the funeral. His French mistress bought him a mahogany coffin. Ten years later, William Cobbett, an English writer who had once denounced Paine but had now become a disciple, visited the burial spot. Cobbett believed that Paine should be buried in England, his birthplace, with a proper monument. So he dug up Paine's bones and took them across the Atlantic. Unable to raise the money for the monument, the bones remained in Cobbett's trunk. After his death, the trunk passed into the hands of his son. When the son was unable to pay his debts, the creditors took over the trunk and the bones. By 1840, the trunk had disappeared. If you are ever in England, examine all old trunks.

Q. When was the first Kentucky Derby run?
A. The first Kentucky Derby was run in May, 1875.

Q. When were the Packard, Peerless, Pierce Arrow, Cadillac, Buick, and Stutz automobiles first made?
A. Packard — 1900; Peerless — 1900; Pierce Arrow — 1901; Cadillac — 1902; Buick — 1904; and Stutz — 1911.

Q. How many states have capitals named after presidents?
A. Four. They are: Madison, Wisconsin; Jefferson City, Missouri; Lincoln, Nebraska; and Jackson, Mississippi.

Q. Who was the first air stewardess, and on what airline did she fly?
A. Ellen Church, who made her first flight on May 15, 1930, between San Francisco, California, and Cheyenne, Wyoming, on United Airlines.

Q. Who was the first black air stewardess?
A. Ruth Taylor, a graduate nurse from Ithaca, New York, who made her first flight on February 11, 1958, from Ithaca to New York City, on Mohawk Airlines.

Q. What was the plane, and who was the pilot of the first plane to exceed the speed of 4,000 miles per hour?

A. The plane was the X-15, flown on November 9, 1961, by Major Robert White at Edwards Air Force Base, California. The plane reached a speed of 4,070 m.p.h. for 86 seconds.

Q. What was the first United States women's college?

A. The first college-level institution for women was the Mount Holyoke Female Seminary, which Mary Lyon opened in South Hadley, Massachusetts in 1837. Mount Holyoke was founded with money collected from 1,800 people in ninety towns. Mrs. Lyon ran the College by severe rules. The first coeducational college was Oberlin College which opened in 1833.

Q. Who was responsible for placing Japanese-Americans in reconcentration centers during World War II?

A. The man responsible was General John L. DeWitt, Commander of the Western Defense Command and the 4th U.S. Army. Acting on Executive Order 9066 issued in February, 1942, by President Franklin Roosevelt, General DeWitt on March 2, 1942 declared California, Oregon, and Washington to be strategic areas. He ordered all persons of Japanese descent removed. About 110,000 persons were sent to camps in California and Arizona. Two-thirds of these people were American born. This action has been called the greatest mass migration of American residents in history. It was greater than any single movement of American Indians from their tribal lands to the reservations. The action of the government was later upheld by the Supreme Court.

Q. When did the mail-order catalogue first appear?

A. Aaron Montgomery Ward and his partner issued the first catalogue in Chicago in 1872. This catalogue consisted of a single sheet of paper.

Q. Daniel Boone is always associated with the history of Kentucky, but where did he spend the last twenty years of his life?

A. In Missouri. Boone (1734-1820) was born near Reading, Pennsylvania, and moved to North Carolina when he was fourteen. He made trips into Kentucky beginning in 1767, and settled there in Boonsborough in 1775. Law suits threatening his lands caused him to leave Kentucky in 1788 and he spent ten years in what is now West Virginia. In 1798 or 1799 he moved to Missouri and spent the rest of his life there. He died in Missouri but his bones were later moved back to Kentucky.

Q. Who invented or established the game of baseball?

A. Baseball is attributed to Colonel Abner Doubleday, who later became a general in the U.S. Army. In 1839 he laid out the first regular baseball diamond at Cooperstown, New York, and formulated the rules of play. The Baseball Hall of Fame is now located in Cooperstown.

Q. Who was Samuel Seabury?

A. Samuel Seabury (1729-1796) was the first bishop of the Episcopal Church in the United States. During the Revolutionary War, Seabury was a Loyalist. He was imprisoned for a short time by the Americans, and later served as a guide and a chaplain for the British army. At the end of the war, he was chosen by the Connecticut clergy to become bishop. He went to England but the bishops there, for political reasons, refused to consecrate him. He then went to Scotland where some non-juring prelates consecrated him on November 14, 1784. In the last years of his life, Seabury avoided political controversies.

Q. Why did John Wesley leave the colony of Georgia?

A. The founder of Methodism had an Anglican parish in Georgia in the 1730s. He fell in love with a young woman but decided not to marry her. When the lady went off to South Carolina to marry another man, Wesley was angry. On the couple's return, Wesley denied them access to communion. The girl's father threatened a law suit, and in 1738 Wesley decided to return to England. His brother, Charles, who had come to Georgia with him, had gone home earlier. Wesley continued to have romantic troubles and, when middle-aged, married a shrew.

Q. When were there only nineteen days in September?

A. In 1752. The American colonies in that month switched from the Julian Calendar to the Gregorian Calendar. Parliament had ordered that the day following September 2nd should be called September 14th. Thus, in order to bring the calendar up to date, eleven days were dropped and the month of September had only nineteen days that year.

Q. Who was the inventor of the American basketball?

A. James Naismith, Springfield, Massachusetts, January 20, 1892.

Q. Who described George Washington as "first in war, first in peace, and first in the hearts of his countrymen"?

A. Henry "Light Horse Harry" Lee, the Revolutionary War General, who spoke these words while giving Washington's funeral eulogy before Congress.

Q. Who was the inventor of the volleyball?

A. William G. Morgan, Holyoke, Massachusetts, 1895.

Q. How many slave traders were executed for violating U.S. laws prohibiting the importation of slaves?

A. One. The foreign slave trade was prohibited in 1808. After 1820, slave trading was regarded as piracy and the penalty was death. On December 20, 1861, Nathaniel Gordon of Portland, Maine, was hanged for slave trading in the Congo. He was the only person in U.S. history to be tried, convicted, and executed for this crime.

Q. How many Chief Justices has the United States had?

A. The United States has had fifteen Chief Justices.

Q. How many rooms are in the White House?

A. The White House has 132 rooms. The official name for the White House is the Executive Mansion.

Q. What was the most important agricultural innovation of the 1930s?

A. The use of hybrid corn. It first became available in 1929 and its use spread rapidly in the 1930s. It resisted certain diseases and it stood up straight — thus it could be machine picked.

Q. Who is a Creole?

A. Originally, a person born in Spanish America of European parents was called a Creole. The name did not imply a person born of racially mixed parents.

Q. Who introduced the log cabin to America?

A. The Swedes, who settled along the Delaware River in the late 1630s. They got the idea of notching logs from the Finns. The early English settlers did not use the log cabin but built homes like those they had back in England.

Q. If you entered the Panama Canal from the easternmost side, you would be entering from which ocean?

A. The Pacific Ocean. The geography of the canal is unusual because the Pacific entrance is east of the Caribbean entrance.

Q. Was Ferdinand Magellan the first man to circumnavigate the earth?

A. No. Magellan was killed in a fight with natives in the Philippines. Part of his crew finished the voyage.

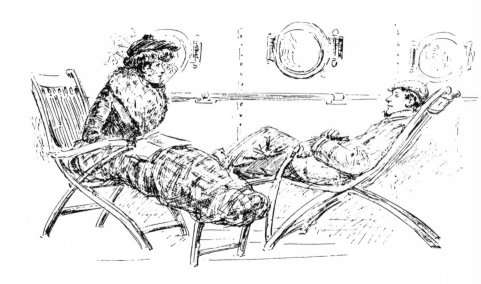

Q. Did the majority of the settlers who arrived on the *Mayflower* come from the Pilgrim groups in the Netherlands?

A. No. Only about one-third of the one hundred passengers on the *Mayflower* came from Holland. The rest were from England. Most of the Pilgrims who left England for the Netherlands remained there.

158

Q. When did the American Medical Association finally recognize that advising patients on contraceptives was a legitimate practice for physicians?

A. In June, 1937. A Supreme court decision one year earlier had eased the federal laws governing contraceptives.

Q. When were the first mines used by American military forces?

A. In January, 1778, in the "Battle of the Kegs." Powder-filled kegs were floated in the Delaware River in an effort to destroy British ships. The mines were not successful. David Bushnell, the inventor of the submarine, devised the plan.

Q. When did the population of the United States reach one hundred million?

A. By 1915.

Q. When did the population of the United States reach two hundred million?

A. By 1969.

Q. When did the idea of a Food Stamp Plan begin?

A. In Rochester, in 1939. By the end of 1940 more than a hundred cities used the plan to get rid of surplus meat, fruit, vegetables, and dairy products. A person on relief who bought one dollar's worth of orange stamps received fifty cents worth of blue stamps free. The stamps were accepted by grocers and eventually redeemed by the city governments.

Q. How did New York Democrats receive the news that their party had nominated William Jennings Bryan for president in 1896?

A. The New Yorkers, most of whom had supported Cleveland and the gold standard, were not too happy. Senator David B. Hill who opposed Bryan put it this way: "I am a Democrat still. Very still."

Q. What happened to the seven Republican senators who joined the Democrats and voted that President Andrew Johnson was not guilty of the impeachment charges against him in 1868?

A. All seven senators failed to win subsequent elections and none held high public office after their current term expired.

Q. What state borders on four of the Great Lakes?

A. Michigan.

Q. What change in communication brought the world to the doorstep of the American farmer?

A. No, it wasn't the telephone. It was Rural Free Delivery, begun by the Post Office Department in 1891 and placed on a regular basis in 1898. R.F.D. brought information and culture to the nation's farmers who then comprised over half of the population.

Q. When was the first "scientific" poll of American public opinion made?

A. The *Pittsburgh Survey* was taken in 1907 and 1908. The Russell Sage Foundation sponsored it — a poll of social views.

160

Q. Who founded *The Reader's Digest?*

A. DeWitt Wallace and his wife, Lila Acheson Wallace, in a basement office in Greenwich Village in February, 1922. Their publication became the most popular magazine in the world.

Q. After the passage of the Income Tax Amendment (the Sixteenth) how tough was the new tax?

A. The first income tax law provided that a married man making $10,000 net income would pay $60 in tax; if he earned a net income of $20,000 his tax would be about $160. Most Americans paid no tax at all.

Q. Who invented condensed milk?

A. Gail Borden received patents for condensed milk in 1856. He founded the Borden Company.

Q. When did the first public high school open?

A. The English High School in Boston opened its doors in 1821. It was designed not for college-preparatory like the old academies, but to prepare boys for careers in business and mechanics.

Q. What was the relation of the Boston Massacre (1770) to "benefit of the clergy"?

A. The two British soldiers convicted of manslaughter for their part in the Boston Massacre of 1770 pleaded benefit of clergy. Under English law the clergy could claim immunity from punishment at the hands of civil officials. Anyone who could prove that he read like a clerk could claim this benefit. Thus the soldiers were burned in the hand instead of being put to death.

Q. What important religious sects were founded in the United States?

A. The United States has produced two native religions — Mormonism (founded by Joseph Smith) and Christian Science (founded by Mary Baker Eddy).

Q. Where was the sales tax first levied?

A. West Virginia introduced a sales tax in 1921. Little interest was shown in the tax in other states until the depression hit. Twenty-one states adopted the sales tax between 1930 and 1935.

Q. Where was the last battle of the Revolutionary War fought?

A. Surprisingly, it appears to have been fought in Arkansas. The battle was fought from April 17 to 24, 1783, at Fort Carlos II (Arkansas Post), Arkansas.

Q. What was the chief motive for Englishmen to move to the New World?

A. Although religion was an important reason, the chief motive appears to be a desire to improve themselves economically.

Q. Did the Pennsylvania Dutch come from Holland?

A. No. They came from Germany and from Switzerland. In German the word "Deutsch" means German. The English-speaking settlers of Pennsylvania thought this word was "Dutch" so the German colonists were misnamed.

Q. Who invented modern air conditioning?

A. Willis H. Carrier. An engineer, Carrier wrote a paper on the theory of air conditioning not long after he graduated from college in 1902. He then began working on the machinery needed. By 1923 he had developed the type of compressor needed for air conditioning.

Q. When were the first actuarial tables for insurance purposes made and by whom?

A. Elizur Wright, "The Father of Life Insurance," drew up the first tables in 1853. Six insurance companies paid Wright $2,000 for his work.

Q. At the beginning of the twentieth century, what was the biggest business in the nation?

A. The United States Steel Company. In 1900, a syndicate headed by J. P. Morgan bought out Andrew Carnegie's steel company and combined it with other interests. The new company was the first billion-dollar corporation. The syndicate that Morgan headed made a profit of sixty million dollars on the deal.

Q. When did commercial air flights to Europe begin?

A. Pan American Airways Dixie Clipper took twenty-two passengers to Lisbon and Marseilles on June 28, 1939. This flight was eventually to reduce and nearly wipe out passenger travel by ships across the Atlantic.

Q. Who invented celluloid?

A. John Wesley Hyatt, in 1873. Celluloid gained new uses in the late 1880s when men like George Eastman began to use it as the basis for camera film.

Q. Who wrote the song, "Home, Sweet Home"?

A. John Howard Payne, an American (1792-1852) wrote the words while traveling in Italy. The music was written by an Englishman, Sir Henry Rowley Bishop. The song was first sung in 1822 as part of an opera. Payne died in Tunis where the American government erected a monument to his memory.

Q. Who invented the pneumatic tire?

A. The pneumatic tire was developed in 1888 by John B. Dunlop. It was first used for bicycles. The idea of rubber tires was much older and was patented by Robert William Thompson in 1845.

Q. Who started the "long drives" from Texas to the cattle towns of Kansas?

A. Joseph G. McCoy in 1867 picked the town of Abilene (which consisted of twelve huts) on the Kansas Pacific railroad, and the long drives, west of the settled areas, began. McCoy should be a candidate for a television series.

Q. When did Nevada legalize gambling?

A. During the Depression in 1931.

Q. What was the date of the founding of the first American law school?

A. The Litchfield Law School at Litchfield, Connecticut, was founded in 1784 by Tapping Reeve. It soon became renowned throughout the nation and its graduates include John C. Calhoun and Aaron Burr.

Q. Who invented Xerox electrostatic copying?

A. Chester F. Carlson of New York in October, 1938. Carlson and his supporters had difficulty in gaining financial support and it was 1960 before the first production-line automatic copier appeared.

Q. What did Georges Clemenceau, the Premier of France, think of President Wilson's fourteen points for a lasting peace?

A. When Clemenceau heard about Wilson's fourteen points, he snapped, "The good Lord was content with ten!"

Q. When was paper money first issued in America?

A. A shortage of specie caused Massachusetts to print an issue of paper money in 1690. This money was used to finance an expedition against the French. The money was issued as bills of credit. At first these bills were not legal tender, but were simply a promise to pay in specie at some future time. The effort was so successful that by 1750 nearly all the colonies had issued some form of paper money. The British then took steps to prevent further issues.

Q. When was the first depression in the United States?

A. At the end of the Revolutionary War. It lasted from 1784 to 1789.

Q. How did the Sears Roebuck Company begin?

A. Richard W. Sears originally had a business selling and repairing watches. One of his employees was Mr. A. C. Roebuck. Sears sold his mail-order business, the R. W. Sears Watch Company, and agreed not to go into business under his own name for at least three years. But he soon got back into business and used the name A. C. Roebuck. At the end of the three years, he changed the name back to Sears, Roebuck, and Company (1893). Mr. Roebuck remained an employee but never had much financial interest in the company.

166

Q. Of the various cattlemen's wars that broke out in the West in the latter half of the nineteenth century, which was the bloodiest?

A. The Lincoln County War in New Mexico in 1878. The war featured one faction led by William H. (Billy the Kid) Bonney. Over sixty men were killed in the Lincoln County War, but only Billy the Kid went on trial. After his conviction the Kid escaped. He was later killed by the Lincoln County sheriff, Pat Garrett.

Q. When were the first silver dollars coined?

A. The first silver dollars were coined by the U.S. Mint in Philadelphia, in 1794.

Q. In the state of Michigan, one city is completely surrounded by another city. What is it called?

A. The city of Hamtramack, an area composed largely of inhabitants whose ancestors came from Poland, is entirely surrounded by the city of Detroit. If you wish to travel from Hamtramack or Detroit to Windsor, Canada, you go south.

167

Q. Who said, "I would rather be right than be President"?
A. Henry Clay, in 1850.

Q. What is the largest concrete structure ever built?
A. The Grand Coulee Dam. It was built in 1942 near Spokane, Washington. It is 550 feet high and 4,300 feet long.

Q. The novelist, Charles Dickens, once referred to an American river as "a slimy monster, hideous to behold." What river was he referring to?
A. Dickens was writing about the Mississippi River. Mark Twain might have disagreed with him.

Q. What state is called the Flat Iron State?
A. The state of Idaho. Although it is the thirteenth largest state, some of its residents claim that it would be the biggest state of all if it were pressed out flat. Officially, it is called the Gem State.

Q. What is the one spot in the United States where four states come together at a single point?
A. The point is where Utah, Arizona, Colorado, and New Mexico meet. Here you could stand in four states at once.

Q. If you wished to go from Los Angeles, California, to Reno, Nevada, which direction would you travel?
A. You would head north — and west. Reno is west of Los Angeles. Check your atlas.

Q. When was the first automobile race held?

A. Probably a race sponsored by a Chicago newspaper in 1895 was the first true race. This was supposed to be an endurance race. The course was 54 miles long. Of the six cars that began, only two finished. Two of the entries were electric, while the others were gasoline-powered. The winner of the race was Charles C. Duryea who finished the course in ten hours and twenty-three minutes, and won $500.

Q. What states make up the area usually referred to as the Midwest?

A. The Midwest is usually regarded as the states of the old Northwest Territory — Ohio, Indiana, Illinois, Michigan, and Wisconsin, plus Minnesota, Iowa, Missouri, Kansas, Nebraska, North Dakota, and South Dakota.

Q. Why was a baseball team named the Dodgers?

A. Supposedly in the late nineteenth century people in Brooklyn were afraid of the new streetcars and began to refer to themselves as "trolley-dodgers." The term "Dodgers" was given to their baseball team which is now located in Los Angeles.

Q. Is the Hudson Bay Company still in the fur business?

A. Although the company has greatly diversified over the centuries, it still buys and sells furs. It has developed into a series of department stores, sells its own brand of Scotch, and has entered the oil business. It is now the third largest retailer in Canada.

Q. When was the first oil boom in the United States?

A. The Senaca Oil Company decided to try to find oil by drilling — a method that had not been used before. They hired Edwin L. Drake to head their project. He set up a derrick near Titusville, Pennsylvania, and after drilling down 69½ feet, hit oil on August 27, 1859. The well produced nine gallons a day and, as soon as the news of Drake's success was learned, the oil boom began.

Q. When was the first transcontinental railroad completed?

A. In the United States, those railroads that run from the Mississippi Valley to the Pacific coast are called transcontinental railroads, even though they only cross two-thirds of the country. Congress authorized the first two railroads — the Central Pacific and the Union Pacific — to meet at Promontory Point, Utah, some fifty miles northwest of Ogden. An engine of each road met there and touched their cowcatchers and the final tie was held in place with a spike of gold. Thus, on May 10, 1869, the nation was united by a railroad.

Q. When did balloon tires first come into use?

A. The Firestone Tire and Rubber Company developed balloon tires in 1923.

Q. When were the first U.S. coins made?
A. The first U.S. coins were minted in 1792.

Q. When did the first electric automobile appear?
A. The first electric automobile was made by William Morris of Des Moines, Iowa, in 1892.

Q. What did Henry Ford originally call the Ford Motor Company?
A. Mr. Ford's first company was the Detroit Automobile Company. The present company evolved from this early one.

Q. Who was the founder of General Motors?
A. William Crapo Durant was building carriages in Flint, Michigan when he gained control of the Buick Company in 1904. He then had the idea of combining a number of automobile companies. By 1910, he had combined a dozen companies, such as Cadillac and Oldsmobile, into a new corporation known as General Motors Company. He even tried at one time to buy out Henry Ford. Durant later lost control of General Motors, regained it, and then lost it a second time.

Q. Was the horse native to America?
A. There were apparently several species of mammals that developed in America and then became extinct. The horse was one of these. The original horse was a tiny animal and disappeared more than ten thousand years ago. When the Spanish arrived in Mexico in the 1500s, they re-introduced the horse.

Q. Who is credited with being the inventor of the self-starter for the automobile?

A. Mr. Charles F. Kettering usually gets the credit for this invention. The first self-starter appeared on Cadillacs in 1911.

Q. Who founded the first ten cent store?

A. Frank W. Woolworth had as one of his early jobs a position in a drygoods store. He worked at a counter where five and ten cent goods were sold. From this experience he got the idea of a store which would sell only goods that cost five and ten cents. He opened the first such store in Utica, New York, in 1879.

Q. When was the first Chamber of Commerce organized?

A. The idea of a Chamber of Commerce apparently originated in Europe as the old guild system died out. A group of merchants in Marseilles, France, set up a Chamber of Commerce as early as 1599. In the United States, the first Chamber of Commerce was organized in New York City in 1768.

Q. When did large chain stores open in the United States?

A. Apparently the first chain store was the Great Atlantic and Pacific Tea Company which opened in 1858. Woolworth's Five and Ten Cent Stores opened its doors in 1879. The Kresge Company was organized in 1885. The United Cigar Stores opened in 1901. J. C. Penney opened his first store in 1902 and the United Drug Company also began that year.

Q. Who started the first department store?

A. Rowland H. Macy began the first department store on Sixth Avenue in New York City in 1858. Wanamaker's in Philadelphia opened in 1861. Marshall Field and Company opened in Chicago in 1881.

Q. It has been claimed that Adolph Hitler once owned 8,960 acres of land in the United States. In what state was this?

A. According to *The People's Almanac*, the property was in the state of Colorado. In 1942, the mayor of Kit Carson, Colorado, claimed that Hitler had inherited this land from German relatives. The land was just outside the city of Kit Carson.

Q. What did Babe Ruth think of his salary when he was paid $80,000 a year?

A. Reporters asked Ruth about the fact that he was making more money during the year than President Hoover. Ruth thought about the question and replied, "Well, I had a better year."

Q. How did the Greyhound Bus Company get its name?

A. Carl E. Wickman, an ex-miner, was trying to sell seven-passenger cars in northern Minnesota in 1914. Wickman had little success in selling the cars so he began to use them as buses to transport people around the area of Hibbing. The buses were a success and Wickman soon expanded his line. He began to add seats to the little buses and someone remarked that they looked like greyhounds. The name stuck and Wickman soon urged his customers to "ride the Greyhound."

Q. How did the Heinz Company develop its "57 Varieties"?

A. Henry J. Heinz got into the produce business in the Pittsburgh area when he was only sixteen. By the time he was twenty-five in 1869, he had formed a partnership and the little company was producing horseradish. Although this company eventually failed, Heinz persisted. By 1876 he had begun the F. & J. Heinz Company. One of his first successful products was ketchup. While in New York, he saw a sign advertising various styles of shoes. He decided that he needed a catchy slogan for his products and settled on "57 Varieties." The company eventually produced far more than 57 products but Heinz retained the slogan that had caught the public's attention.

Q. The United States shares all of the five Great Lakes, except one, with Canada. Which lake is the exception?

A. Lake Michigan is the only one of the Great Lakes entirely within the United States.

Q. What state claimed to be an independent republic before it finally joined the Union?

A. The state of Vermont. Both New Hampshire and New York claimed the land between the Connecticut River and Lake Champlain. These claims were opposed by the Allen brothers — Ethan, Levi, and Ira — who set up a government in 1777 and established the army of "Green Mountain Boys" to protect the independence of the area. They even promised the British that the region would be neutral during the Revolutionary War if their independence were recognized. Although settlers came into the area in increasing numbers, the Allens talked of a separate treaty with the British to protect their interests. Finally, the Vermonters settled their quarrel with New York and after fourteen years as a quasi-independent republic, Vermont became the fourteenth state in 1791.

Q. Where was the first skyscraper built?

A. Chicago. The Home Insurance Company Building, ten stories high with a steel skeleton, was designed by William Jenney. Construction began in 1884 and the building was completed in the autumn of 1885. The steel frame carried the weight of the walls and the floors. Since the masonry bore no weight, the building could be raised to heights never dreamed of before. Chicago soon became the leading city for skyscrapers.

Q. Who invented Coca-Cola?

A. An Atlanta, Georgia, druggist, John S. Pemberton, developed a formula for Coca-Cola in 1886. One of his friends suggested the name which was derived from the two chief components of the drink, the leaves of the coca bush and the nuts of the cola tree. At first the Coca-Cola Company opposed the popular name of "Coke." When the public continued to demand "Coke," the company finally registered the name in 1920. The drink is one of the most popular soft-drinks in the world, but the formula remains a closely guarded secret.

Q. Who invented ice cream?

A. The national committee in charge of the celebration of the bicentennial of George Washington's birth reported in 1932 that he had invented ice cream. In Washington's expense record of May, 1784, a "cream machine for ice" is mentioned. The first commercial ice cream was advertised in New York City in 1786.

Q. Was the Pony Express Company a success?

A. No. The freight company known as the Central Overland, California & Pike's Peak Express had a contract to carry mail between Salt Lake City and Placerville, California. They hoped to win enough attention through publicity to win a mail subsidy from the government. So in 1860 one of the owners, William Russell, conceived the idea of a pony express from the Missouri River to California. Riders were to exchange horses every ten miles and at first, each rider would cover thirty miles.

The first rider left St. Joseph, Missouri on April 3, 1860. On April 13, just one hour under ten days, the mail arrived in San Francisco. The company soon had eighty men — forty riding in each direction. Soon men were riding 75 to 100 miles, and Buffalo Bill Cody once rode 320 miles in a stretch. The riders did this for a salary ranging from $50 to $150 a month.

The company soon lowered its costs from $5 to $2 a half-ounce, but estimated their actual cost at $38 to deliver each piece of mail. Then on October 24, 1861, the Pacific coast was linked to the East by telegraph. After only sixteen months, the Pony Express folded. The company was taken over by Wells, Fargo & Company in 1866.

Q. Who invented the ferris wheel?

A. The ferris wheel was invented by George Ferris in 1892. He wanted an attraction for the Columbian Exposition that was to be held in Chicago in 1893. The wheel that he developed was 264 feet high. It had thirty-six cars, each of which could carry sixty passengers. The ferris wheel was an enormous success.

Q. New York City has two stock exchanges. Why?

A. The New York Stock Exchange started in 1792 as a protective league of brokers. In 1817 the New York Stock Exchange began in roughly its present form. Some speculators, who did not belong to the New York Exchange, stayed close to it and traded outdoors in what was called a "curb" market. By 1912, the New York Curb Exchange was organized and by 1921 they moved out of the street and into a building. In 1953 the old curb exchange became the American Stock Exchange.

Q. Who was the first person to be killed in the crash of an airplane?

A. On September 17, 1908, a plane carrying Orville Wright and Thomas Selfridge hit a wire at Fort Myer, Virginia. Selfridge, who was in the army, was killed and Wright injured his hip and leg.

Q. When was the American Red Cross organized?

A. Clara Barton organized the American Red Cross in Washington, D.C., on May 21, 1881. Miss Barton had served as a nurse in the Civil War and had helped with relief during the Franco-Prussian War. Here she was associated with the International Red Cross which had been set up by an international agreement at Geneva in 1864. She succeeded in having the United States sign the Geneva agreement in 1882. Miss Barton served as president of the American Red Cross until 1904.

Q. Who said, "Don't fire unless fired upon; but if they mean to have war, let it begin here"?

A. These words are attributed to Captain John Parker, who led the minutemen in the Battle of Lexington, April 19, 1775.

Q. Who said, "You must obey this, now, for a law — that he that will not work shall not eat"?

A. Captain John Smith in Jamestown, Virginia, September, 1608. Smith, then president of the Council in Virginia, was determined to lower the colony's terrible death rate. He enforced his rule with vigor, but he was not as tough as he sounds. He only expected his people to work six hours a day. During his time in office, the death rate was significantly lower than afterward.

179

Q. Who said, "You may fire when you are ready, Gridley"?

A. Commodore George Dewey on board the *Olympia* in Manila Bay, May 1, 1898, gave the order to Captain Charles V. Gridley. The battle destroyed the Spanish fleet in the Philippines.

Q. Who said, "They see nothing in the rule that to the victors belong the spoils of the enemy"?

A. Senator William L. Marcy (1786-1857) in a speech on the Senate floor in January, 1832. Marcy used these words to defend Martin Van Buren against an attack by Henry Clay. The term "the spoils system" stuck to the administrative practices of President Andrew Jackson.

Q. Whose dying words were, "Now comes the mystery"?

A. These were the last words of the Rev. Henry Ward Beecher, the nineteenth century preacher and reformer. Beecher died on March 8, 1887.

Q. Who took a fortress by saying, "Surrender in the name of the great Jehovah and the Continental Congress"?

A. Colonel Ethan Allen (1739-89) is supposed to have uttered these words in demanding that the British surrender Fort Ticonderoga on May 10, 1775. The British commander was asleep when Allen, Benedict Arnold, and some Green Mountain Boys surrounded the fort. Another version has it that Allen (who was no friend to organized religion) yelled at the British officer, "Come out you damned rat."

181

Q. Who was the first American to make a flight into space?

A. Commander Alan Shepard was carried into space for a fifteen-minute flight on May 5, 1961. The space capsule was carried by a Redstone missile. Shepard flew for 302 miles after the launching at Cape Canaveral. He reached a speed of 4500 miles an hour and an altitude of 115 miles. For five minutes, Shepard was weightless.

Q. How did the Smith Brothers get into the cough drop business?

A. Andrew and William Smith were the sons of a restaurant owner in Poughkeepsie, New York. A customer in the restaurant gave their father a recipe for a candy that was useful for curing coughs. The family began to manufacture and advertise the remedy that they made in their kitchen. When the father died in 1886, Andrew and William found that they had many competitors, many of whom used names similar to theirs. To distinguish their product from other brands, the brothers began to put their pictures on the packages. The portraits of the bearded brothers soon became a distinct American trademark.

Q. Who invented the cash register?

A. James Ritty of Dayton, Ohio. Ritty ran a restaurant and saloon and thought that his help was making off with the profits. He suffered a breakdown and took a trip to Europe to recover. While aboard ship, he noticed a device that kept a record of the revolutions of the propeller shaft. He decided to devise a machine to keep track of the sales in his business. In 1879, Ritty and his brother patented their first cash register, and they soon improved it so that the amount of the sale popped up to be seen by the customer as well as the employee. Ritty thought this

182

would end pilfering. Ritty and his brother had little success in manufacturing the machines, so in 1884 he sold the patents for $1,000. The new National Cash Register Company added a cash drawer, a bell, and a system whereby the machine kept a record of all transactions. The company was a great success.

Q. Who introduced ready-to-eat breakfast foods to the American public?

A. The credit probably should go to Charles William Post. In 1897 he began producing Grape Nuts. In 1915, he introduced Post Toasties and in 1922 Post Bran Flakes. General Foods now produces these products.

Bibliography

Allen, Frederick L. *The Big Change*. New York: Harper & Row, 1952.

Bailey, Thomas A. *Presidential Greatness*. New York: Appleton Century, 1966.

Bailey, Thomas A. *Probing America's Past: A Critical Examination of Major Myths and Misconceptions*. Two vols. Lexington, Mass.: D.C. Heath and Company, 1973.

Banner, Hubert S. *Calamities of the World*. Detroit: Tower Books, 1971.

Barker, James D. *The Presidential Character: Predicting Performance in the White House*. Englewood, N.J.: Prentice-Hall, Inc., 1972.

Billington, Ray Allen. *The Far Western Frontier, 1830-1860*. New York: Harper & Brothers, 1956.

Bombaugh, Charles C. *Facts and Fancies for the Curious*. Philadelphia, 1905.

Boorstin, Daniel J. *The Americans: The Colonial Experience*. New York: Random House, 1958.

Boorstin, Daniel J. *The Americans: The National Experience*. New York: Random House, 1965.

Boorstin, Daniel J. *The Americans: The Democratic Experience*. New York: Random House, 1973.

Boorstin, Daniel J. *The Image*. New York: Atheneum, 1962.

Branch, E. Douglas. *The Sentimental Years, 1836-1860*. New York: Hill and Wang, 1965.

Brewer, Ebenezer C. *Brewer's Dictionary of Phrase and Fable*. Revised by Dvor H. Evans. New York: Harper and Row, 1970.

Burke's *Presidential Families of the United States of America*. London: Burke's Peerage Limited, 1975.

Campbell, Hannah, *Why Did They Name It*, New York: Ace Books, 1964.

Carlinsky, Dan and Edwin Goodgold. *Trivia and More Trivia*. N. P.: Castle Books, 1975.

Carruth, Gorton and Associates. *The Encyclopedia of American Facts and Dates*. Sixth Edition. New York: Thomas Y. Crowell Company, 1972.

Editors of American Heritage. *The American Heritage Pictorial Atlas of United States History*. New York: American Heritage Publishing Co., 1966.

Editors of American Heritage. *The American Heritage Pictorial History of the Presidents of the United States*. Two vols. New York: American Heritage Publishing Co.

Edwards, Eliezer. *Words, Facts, and Phrases*. Philadelphia, 1881. Republished by Gale Research Company, Detroit, 1968.

Ewing, Cortez. *The Judges of the Supreme Court, 1789-1937*. Minneapolis: The University of Minnesota Press, 1938.

Felton, Bruce and Mark Fowler. *Felton & Fowler's Best, Worst, and Most Unusual*. New York: Thomas Y. Crowell Co., 1975.

Fogg, Walter. *One Thousand Sayings of History Presented as Pictures in Prose*. Boston: 1929. Republished by Gryphon Books, Ann Arbor, 1971.

Frank, Sid. *The Presidents: Tidbits and Trivia*. Maplewood, N.J.: Hammond Inc., 1975.

Funk, Charles E. and Charles E. Funk, Jr. *Horsefeathers and Other Curious Words*. New York: Harper Brothers, 1958.

Garrison, William B. *Why You Say It*. Nashville: Abingdon Press, 1955.

Ginger, Ray. *Age of Excess: The United States from 1877 to 1914*. New York: The Macmillan Company, 1965.

Ginger, Ray. *Ray Ginger's Jokebook about American History*. New York: New Viewpoints, 1974.

Haskins, Frederick J. *5,000 New Answers to Questions*. New York, 1933.

Hess, Stephen. *America's Political Dynasties*. Garden City, N.Y.: Doubleday & Co., 1966.

Jensen, Merrill. *The New Nation*. New York: Vintage Books, 1950.

Johnson, Thomas Herbert. *The Oxford Companion to American History*. New York: Oxford University Press, 1966.

Jones, Robert M. *Can Elephants Swim?* New York: Time-Life Books, 1969.

Kane, Joseph Nathan. *Facts About Presidents*. Third Edition. New York: N.W. Wilson Co., 1974.

Kane, Joseph Nathan. *Famous First Facts*. Third Edition. New York: H.W. Wilson, Co., 1964 and 1974.

Laughlin, William H. *Laughlin's Fact Finder: People, Places, Things, Events*. Chicago and New York: Parker Publishing Co., 1969.

McWhiter, Norris and Ross McWhiter. *Dunlop Illustrated Encyclopedia of Facts*. Garden City, N.Y.: Doubleday & Co., 1970.

Menendez, Albert. *The American Political Quiz Book*. New York: Drake Publishers, 1975.

Miller, Hope Ridings. *Scandals in the Highest Office: Facts and Fictions in the Private Lives of Our Presidents*. New York: Random House, 1973.

Miller, Merle. *Plain Speaking: An Oral Biography of Harry S. Truman*. New York: G. P. Putnam's Sons, 1973.

Morris, Dan and Inez Morris. *Who Was Who in American Politics*. New York: Hawthorn Books, Inc., 1974.

Nye, Russel B. *A Baker's Dozen*. East Lansing, Mich.: Michigan State University Press, 1965.

Passell, Peter, and Leonard Ross. *The Best*. New York: Farrar, Straus, and Giroux, 1974.

Peckham, Howard H., ed. *The Toll of Independence*. Chicago: The University of Chicago Press, 1974.

Peoples Bicentennial Commission. *Quiz Book of the American Revolution*. New York: Bantam Books, 1975.

Saltz, Donald. *The Bantam Trivia Quiz Book*. New York: Bantam Books, Inc., 1975.

Schemmer, Benjamin F. and others. *Almanac of Liberty: A Chronology of American Military Anniversaries from 1775 to the Present*. New York: Macmillan Publishing Co., Inc., 1974.

Shankle, George E. *American Nicknames: Their Origin and Significance*. 2nd ed., New York: The H. W. Wilson Co., 1955.

Smith, Don. *Peculiarities of the Presidents*. Van Wert, Ohio: 1938.

Sobel, Robert. *Biographical Directory of the United States Executive Branch, 1774-1971*. Westport, Conn.: Greenwood Publishing Co., 1971.

Taylor, Tim. *The Book of Presidents*. New York: Arno Press, 1972.

Time, the editors of. *Live Them Again*. New York: Simon and Schuster, 1953.

Wallace, Irving. *The Square Pegs: Some Americans who Dared to be Different*. New York: Alfred A. Knopf, 1957.

Wallechinsky, David and Irving Wallace. *The People's Almanac*. Garden City, N.Y.: Doubleday and Co., Inc., 1975.

Webster's Biographical Dictionary. Springfield, Mass.: G. & D. Merriam Co., 1943.

Whitney, David C. *The American Presidents*. Garden City, N.Y.: Doubleday and Co., Inc., 1969.

Wilson, Vincent, Jr. *The Book of the Presidents*. Silver Springs, Md.: American History Research Assoc., 1962.

Picture Credits

The drawings and illustrations that appear in this book are from the following sources:

The Encyclopedia of Small Spot Engravings, Phoenix, Arizona: Valley of the Sun Publishing Company.

Old Engravings and Illustrations, Vols. I and II, Minneapolis, Minnesota: The Dick Sutphen Studio, 1968.

Handbook of Early Advertising Art, New York: Dover Publications, Inc. 1956.

An Old-Fashioned Christmas in Illustration and Decoration, New York: Dover Publications, Inc. 1970.